Living with Wolfdogs

An Everyday Guide to
a Lifetime Companionship

Nicole Wilde

Living with Wolfdogs

ISBN 0-9667726-4-4

Photo credits:
Rachel Nolan p. 8
Jim Malcolm p.18
Monty Sloan pp. 35, 61, 86
Diane Horne pp. 48, 70
Jill Moore p.75

Back cover photo top by Madeleine.
Back cover photo bottom by Gail Whitford.

Cover photo of Spirit and all other uncredited photographs
were taken by the author.

Diagrams pp. 50, 51 & 55 by C.C. Wilde

I would like to thank:

Ian Dunbar for his guidance, encouragement and humor; my parents for their support; Monty Sloan, World Class Wolf-Pretzler, for his input; all those knowledgeable folks who patiently answered questions when I first started out and let me visit with their packs; and my country-wide network of wolf-loving friends, who my husband laughingly refers to as the "Wolf Mafia." You know who you are.

Last but definitely not least, special thanks to my husband, C.C., for putting up with the constant calls and animal-related craziness, sharing me with the four-leggeds (and often seeing me less than they do) and for being the incredibly wonderful person he is.

---

*This book is dedicated
to the four-leggeds
and to those who put their
hearts and souls
into caring for them.*

---

*...and to Sequoia, my
Little Roo Girl,
1991-2004.*

The term "wolf hybrid" does not appear in this book. Although it has been in common use for years, it is technically incorrect. In 1993, the Smithsonian re-classified dogs (formerly *canis familiaris*) as *canis lupus familiaris*, a sub-species of wolf, *canis lupus*. Since "hybrid" implies a cross of two different species, under this new classification the term "wolf hybrid" is incorrect. (The debate about what separates one species from another is still up in the air. Though most wolf biologists seem to agree with the reclassification, not all do.)

For ease of reading, wolfdogs are referred to herein as "he" and felines as "she."

Table of Contents

Foreword

Many years ago, there was an internet chat group that focused on wolfdogs. Participating in the ongoing discussion were wolfdog owners, trainers and rescuers, along with others who were simply fascinated by these beautiful animals and wanted to learn more. Because I frequently offered on-list advice, I began to receive private requests for help. Although happy to comply, I was soon spending over two hours a day answering wolfdog-related queries. At the time, there were very few resources in print regarding wolfdogs. So I wrote *Living with Wolfdogs*.

It has been almost ten years since the book was written. I would like to report that since that time, much has changed in the public's perception and knowledge regarding wolfdogs. I would like to—but I can't. There are still many breeders who do not educate prospective owners about the realities of living with a semi-exotic animal; still too many people who think it would be "cool" to have an animal that is part wolf, and get one without further thought; and unfortunately, there are still too few places for an unwanted wolfdog to live out its life.

This second edition is both a revision and an expansion of the original text. It reflects the knowledge and experience I have acquired in the past decade as a wolfdog owner/rescuer and professional dog trainer/behavior specialist. To those who are considering a wolfdog as a pet, thank you for taking the time to research the subject. To those who are already sharing your lives with these unique companions, I hope this book will give you the knowledge and support you need to make your relationship a success.

Nicole Wilde

*This handsome white German Shepherd
mix has just a bit of Arctic wolf in him.*

Introduction

So What *is* a Wolfdog, Exactly? Are they Good Pets?

The issue of wolfdogs as pets is a hot one. Those who are opposed can be vehement in their hatred of any animal that has "wolf blood," harking back to that age-old superstitious fear of the wolf. Others feel an animal that is partly exotic has no place in the home. Even among those who are in favor of wolfdog "ownership" (wolfdogs are more of a companion than a pet to be "owned"), there is disagreement as to what wolfdogs are like. Do they make good guard dogs? Are they untrainable? Must they live in outdoor enclosures? (*No, no* and *it depends.*) These questions will be answered differently by wolfdog owners, based on their experiences with their own animals. The danger in generalizing one's own experience to wolfdogs as a whole is that it does not yield an accurate overall picture. There can be vast variations in appearance, temperament and other characteristics from one wolfdog to the next. It is easy to see how this disparity, along with the subjective nature of personal experience, can make it difficult to come to a consensus as to what wolfdogs are like and whether they make good pets.

Having rescued, lived with, trained and visited with hundreds of wolfdogs over the years, I have seen everything from the best to the worst case scenarios. Based on that cumulative experience, I will attempt to describe what wolfdogs are really like.

> *Wolfdogs are not normally the result of a wild wolf mating with a pet dog; they are almost always the offspring of two animals bred in captivity.*

Breed Standards

For every breed of dog there exists a breed standard—
a set of parameters for physical appearance and behavior that
describes the ideal for that particular breed. If I were to say,
"Cocker Spaniel," you could envision the dog to which I was
referring. You know what a Cocker Spaniel looks like, and unless
the animal was poorly bred, you would also have an idea of the
temperament. *There is no widely accepted "breed standard" for
wolfdogs*, which is one of the major reasons it is difficult and
often inaccurate to make blanket statements about them. When I
say "wolfdog," I could be describing any mix resulting from the
breeding of dog to wolf, dog to wolfdog, wolfdog to wolfdog, or
wolfdog to wolf; it could be a mix of any sub-species of wolf
crossed with any breed of dog. (Malamute, Husky and German
Shepherd are the most common.) While many wolfdogs share
physical traits such as a tall, lanky build, a bushy tail that hangs

Sissy is approximately half wolf

rather than curls, large feet, elongated snout and slanted eyes, there is a vast difference in looks and behavior between a wolfdog that is mostly Malamute and a wolfdog that is mostly wolf. They are, however, both legitimately wolfdogs.

Percentages/Generation/Wolf Content

Another complicating factor in trying to describe wolfdogs is that many sold by breeders are stated to be of higher wolf content than they actually are. This may be due to the fact that the breeder does not know the accurate percentages in her own lines; or it could be a simple case of more wolf equals more money. Although there are recognized wolf hybrid registries and some legitimate breeders, unscrupulous breeders have been known to form their own registries, proudly providing papers with purchase that trace the wolfdog's purported lineage. More often than not, those papers would be best used at the bottom of a bird cage! Thanks to those breeders, many owners believe they have a much higher content wolfdog than they actually do.

The danger in someone with a wolfdog of over-represented wolf content telling others how easy it is to live with a high content wolfdog or pure wolf is that those listening might get a legitimate high content wolfdog—and boy, are they in for a surprise! Or the person with the animal of over-represented wolf content might eventually get a legitimate high content wolfdog and be totally unprepared for the differences. *More wolf content does not equal a better pet.* Anyone who goes around bragging about his "wolf" is only putting his companion in danger and making himself look foolish. What's the danger? If your wolfdog is ever involved in causing harm to a person or animal, or is impounded at the shelter as a stray, you might not get him back. Accidents happen, legalities exist, and when a "wolf" is involved, that animal often ends up euthanized.

Calculating Percentages

The percentage of wolf in a wolfdog is calculated by adding together the percentage of wolf in each parent, then dividing by two. For example, a 75% wolfdog mated to a 25% wolfdog would produce pups that are 50% wolf, since 75 plus 25 equals 100, divided by two equals 50.

Discussing exact percentages in wolfdogs can be misleading. Even when a pure wolf is bred to a pure dog, there can be significant variation in physical appearance—phenotype—within the litter. When this disparity is obvious, e.g., half the pups are much lighter in color than the others, it is referred to as a "gene split" in the litter. There will also be behavioral variations. Some pups will show higher levels of characteristic wolfish traits such as shyness or "skittishness," while others will be more outgoing. But regardless of these differences, the actual designated percentage of wolf will be the same.

Generation - What's all this "F1" Stuff?

To further complicate matters, there is the question of how many generations away a wolfdog is from a pure wolf. "F_1" or "first generation" is a term commonly used to refer to a wolfdog that has at least one pure wolf parent. An F_2 or "second generation" wolfdog would be two generations away from pure (i.e., a grandparent is a pure wolf) and so on. In general, the higher the F number (the more generations away from pure wolf), the "doggier" the animal will be in looks and behavior.

Rather than citing percentages and generation, for our purposes, we will refer to wolfdogs as "low content" (very little wolf content, 1-39%), "mid content" (close to half wolf, approximately 40-74%) or "high content" (mostly wolf, 75-98%). The photos included throughout this book will give you a rough idea of what legitimate low, mid and high content wolfdogs look like.

> *"98% wolf" is a term often used by those with pure wolves, to avoid legal hassles.*

In My Humble Opinion

A personal note before we move on... Years ago, I co-ran a rescue center in southern California. We cared for over thirty adult canines; some were wolfdogs and some, pure wolves. The overwhelming majority had come to us between the ages of one and two years, as they were becoming sexually mature and beginning to act, well...wolfy! Their owners were unprepared for the behavior of these "pets" and decided they could no longer deal with them. At the rescue center, they were loved and cared for, for the rest of their lives.

Personally, there is nothing that makes me happier than sitting in the dirt, rubbing a wolfy tummy and singing "Who's Afraid of the Big Bad Wolf," both of us grinning away like fools. If you ask me, one hour of that is worth five hours of therapy! That said, I also have to state that *wolfdogs are not the perfect pet for the average person*, and finding homes for them after this is discovered too late is a major challenge. There is an incredibly high number of unwanted wolfdogs, yet most people do not realize the scope of the problem.

At the rescue center, we received at least five calls per day from people wanting to relinquish their wolfdogs. That number doubled during the spring and summer months. Women explained how their husbands had wanted an exotic animal for their own macho reasons, then found they could not handle that animal. Parents called to say their kids had gone off to college or moved, leaving the wolfdog behind. Then there were those who had bred their wolfdogs but could not place all the pups.

There are many reasons animals are given up. Even dogs that are not part wolf have behaviors their owners find problematic. But those behaviors, e.g., digging, chewing, nipping, yard escaping and destruction, are often exaggerated in the wolfdog. Many people are not willing nor are they equipped to deal with them. That is why most wolfdog rescues are filled to capacity, and unfortunately, a large number of those callers end up euthanizing their animals.

If you are planning to breed your wolfdog, please reconsider. Even if you found good homes for the pups, you would have no

Tabitha - very high wolf content

control over what happened as they grew up. If adopters were eventually unable to keep the pups, would you be willing to take them back? A responsible breeder would, and it would state so in their contract. Otherwise, the pups could end living their lives out at a rescue or being euthanized. Finding new homes for adult wolfdogs is more of a challenge than you might think. And what if the pups you placed were then bred? Think about how many unwanted wolfdogs you might be responsible for down the line.

There are those who have been breeding wolfdogs professionally for many years. They know the genetic background, temperament and appearance of their lines. They do not breed haphazardly just because "the pups would be adorable;" neither should you. If you have mature wolfdogs who could potentially mate, get them spayed or neutered. You will not only be preventing unwanted litters of pups, but will lower your wolfdogs' chances of developing diseases such as testicular or mammary cancer. Neutering also helps to curb male-male canine aggression and the desire to roam when a female in heat is in the area.

Whether anyone should be breeding wolfdogs at this time is another issue altogether. As a rescue person, my vote would be a moritorium on breeding wolfdogs until the current overpopulation situation eases and a workable breed standard can be created. That might sound harsh, but as someone who truly loves these animals, I do not want to see any more suffering.

In the meantime, there are knowledgeable, responsible wolfdog owners out there, and I would encourage anyone who chooses to have a wolfdog to be just that.

What to Consider
When Considering a Wolfdog

Why a Wolfdog?

There are many factors to consider before jumping into wolfdog ownership. First, think long and hard about *why* you want an animal that is part wolf. If you are experienced with dogs, have done your research, and understand the time and effort involved in sharing your life with these beautiful, intelligent, sometimes challenging companions, great. But be honest. Examine your motivations to be sure you do not want a wolfdog for the wrong reasons. It is understandably tempting to get a gorgeous, exotic creature to show off to others. Who wouldn't appreciate the oohs and aahs of onlookers as you walk your lanky, wild-looking companion down the street? But as with humans, relationships based on looks alone do not usually fare well once the infatuation phase has passed. Besides, the more wolfy-looking the animal, the more wolfy-acting, which can translate into serious behavior issues that can be difficult to handle.

Some people feel that by having an animal that is part wolf, they can "own" a piece of the wild. But as any wolfdog owner will tell you, the incredible amount of time and effort involved in sharing one's life with a wolfdog inevitably makes it feel as though the wolfdog owns you! Then there are those who believe the wolf is their spiritual totem animal, so they long to share their life with one. While I have a solemn respect for that spiritual belief system, there is a *big* difference between a wolf on the astral plane and a wolf in your living room. For one thing, your spirit guide is not as likely to eat holes in your couch!

Beagles are Legal, What About Wolfdogs?

In some states, wolfdogs are perfectly legal; in others, they are absolutely illegal. Some states allow wolfdogs of a certain percentage or less, while others allow ownership if a permit is obtained. Laws can vary from county to county within the same state. Take the time to research legalities in your area. Why are legalities so important? Because in a wolfdog-banned area, if your wolfdog gets out of your yard, you might not get him back. Double those odds if he injures a neighbor's animal or is even suspected of posing a threat. Your local Department of Animal Control is a good place to start. Make an anonymous call and ask about the laws in your area. Repeat the inquiry at various times to verify the information with different officers; very often wolfdog ownership is a grey area about which animal control workers are not well informed.

Home is Where the Pack Is

The next consideration is your lifestyle. Do you honestly have enough time to devote to a very social, pack-oriented companion? If you and your spouse work full-time outside the home and plan to leave your wolfdog home alone five days a week, please reconsider. Early socialization and training are critical to a pup's development. This life stage in particular will require a *lot* of your time and attention. It's like having an infant! Even in adulthood, wolfdogs need attention. Those isolated in back yards all day can become bored and extremely destructive, and many quickly become accomplished escape artists. They are also likely to howl, which will not make you popular with your neighbors and might even incur the wrath of Animal Control.

Do you take frequent business trips? Wolfdogs bond so closely with their owners that yours will probably be miserable for prolonged periods away from you. Does your family vacation now and then? Be aware that some boarding kennels will not accept wolfdogs and many do not have the proper facilities to house them (i.e., escape-proof, covered pens). Is there someone you could count on to watch your wolfdogs while you are away? Now is the time to consider and prepare for those situations.

If you work full-time and already have a wolfdog who is left alone daily, consider providing a canine companion. It does not necessarily need to be another wolfdog—a dog of comparable size and complimentary temperament, preferably of the opposite sex, will do. I do not know of any breed of dog that enjoys isolation, but it does seem to be particularly hard on wolfdogs.

A wolfdog owner's definition of "house broken"

Marigolds vs. Moon Craters

About your back yard: How attached are you to those flower beds? A wolfdog is a poor choice for those who have immaculate landscaping and intend to keep it that way. If you can live with a landscape of dirt and moon craters, great. If not, think again. Now, I am assuming here that you have a yard. I have known people who lived in apartments and got wolfdogs; those are the same people who ended up phoning a rescue center, desperate to give up their animal. *Wolfdogs are not suited for apartment living, period.* They need room to run and can become extremely destructive when left alone in a small, confined environment. While a pet dog might get bored and chew your slippers, I personally know of numerous wolfdogs who have eaten holes in couches, torn up linoleum, and even eaten through dry wall when left alone in apartments. Will they all do this? No. Are they capable of it? Oh, yes. Do you really want to take that chance?

"Paging Houdini..."

Before leaving your yard, let's discuss containment. What type of fencing do you have? Standard chain link fencing is six feet high—not a challenge for most wolfdogs to scale. Even a pure Husky can get over a six-foot wall without much effort. If your current fencing is not adequate to contain a wolfdog, read the section on containment and decide whether you want to invest the necessary time, effort and money to upgrade. *Proper containment is a must.* I cannot emphasize this point strongly enough. Proper containment can literally save your wolfdog's life. Some people consider a chain to be "containment." *Chaining an animal is* never *acceptable as a primary, permanent means of containment.* Any chained animal could become frustrated and injure itself trying to break free. A chained dog could easily become possessive of the small, surrounding chain-delineated territory, setting the stage for a tragic "accident" should anyone invade that space. This is a classic scenario in which children have been bit by wolfdogs, and is wholly avoidable.

Getting To Know You

Hope you don't mind if we get personal for a moment. Are you married or living with someone? If so, how does that person feel about sharing space with a wolfdog? If you sense any opposition, don't get one. Someone who is not crazy about the idea to begin with is apt to become even less enthused with each accident or incident that occurs; and believe me, there will be many. It takes love, patience, and a great sense of humor to live successfully with a wolfdog. If you do not have 100% commitment from your partner, your chances of success are low.

Continuing on a personal note, what are your plans for the next ten to fifteen years? Wolfdogs in captivity have approximately the same lifespan as most large domestic dogs. If you are at a point in your life where the present is unstable or the future uncertain (e.g., you are considering going away to college or moving to another state, are financially unstable or in the midst of a divorce), do not get a wolfdog at this time. Wait until your life settles down and you can make a long-term commitment. What about children? Perhaps you do not currently have children and are not planning to have them in the immediate future. But what about a few years down the road? Calls from people who tearfully explain, "We have a baby now so the wolfdog has to go" are all too common. If you plan to have children and anticipate a wolfdog becoming a problem at that time, don't get a wolfdog.

Strange, Small Two-Legged Creatures

Let's talk for a moment about children and dogs—not wolfdogs, just plain old dogs. Many rescues and shelters will not adopt dogs out to families with children under six years of age. Their logic is that young children cannot be counted upon to interact safely with dogs. A child teasing or slapping a dog might elicit a growl or snap, and rightly so. Children are also likely to make sudden sounds or movements that can scare dogs. Even if a dog is not acting defensively, any large canine is capable of injuring a child by simply knocking them down or playing too roughly. Of course, no young child should be left alone unsupervised with any dog, even for a moment.

Now let's consider wolfdogs. Wolfdogs are commonly a mix of wolf and Malamute, German Shepherd or Husky. Male wolfdogs average 80-90 pounds; weights of 100 pounds or more are not uncommon. Females weigh 60-85 pounds on average. Any animal of that size and strength certainly has the potential to injure a small child, even accidentally. Then there is the question of prey drive. Wolves have a stronger prey drive than most dogs. In the wild, a small animal running or squealing is likely to elicit a prey response. With wolfdogs, movement and crying can trigger prey drive. In the Los Angeles area, the majority of reported cases of wolfdogs attacking children in the 1990s involved a child moving past on a skateboard, bicycle, or running. (Info courtesy of West Valley Animal Care & Control, Chatsworth, CA.) In each case, movement

Mattea -
very high wolf content

triggered prey drive. (Of course, had the owners had proper containment, those accidents could have been avoided.) This is not meant to give the impression that all wolfdogs will "hunt" small children. However, because of the reasons mentioned here, combined with a wolf's lightning-fast reflexes, *wolfdogs are not recommended for families with small children.* Care should always be taken with wolfdogs in public places, particularly off-leash dog parks, especially when children are present. If you have a wolfdog, letting him off-leash in public is putting him at risk; if he hurts another dog or person, even in self-defense, he is the one who will suffer.

Other Considerations

Wolfdogs have been known to chase and kill cats, bunnies, birds, horses, livestock and smaller dogs. If you have any of these living with you, consider carefully the temperaments of all concerned before you bring a wolfdog into your home. Will *all* wolfdogs go after small animals? No. Many wolfdogs live peaceably side by side with other animals, especially if raised together. (See *Compatibility/Integrating your Pack*). Others do not.

Are you looking for a house dog who will curl up on the couch with you to watch *White Fang*? While many low and some mid content wolfdogs can live in the house, the majority of true high contents end up living in outdoor enclosures. If they come indoors at all, the visits are carefully supervised. Of course, a high content wolfdog can live in the house as a pup—so could a baby mountain lion. But as they mature, many high content wolfdogs cause so much destruction that their owners decide something must be done. If an outdoor enclosure cannot be built, that "something" is often to relinquish the animal to a rescue or shelter. There are a few hardy souls who live with high content wolfdogs indoors.

However, most have made significant compromises in their living arrangements. If you are the type who collects fragile knickknacks and likes an immaculate house, do not get a wolfdog of any percentage.

Homeowners should be aware that many insurance companies will not insure a home that houses wolfdogs. Breed-specific legislation is becoming common in many states, and certain breeds have been designated as potentially dangerous. Wolfdogs are almost always on that list. A quick call to your insurance company can help you to ascertain whether there are canine-specific limitations on homeowner's insurance for your area.

Although it might not seem like a major factor, consider your financial situation. Feeding a large dog can be costly. A forty-pound bag of quality kibble can cost thirty dollars or more. Veterinary care is another expense, from checkups, vaccinations, infections, allergies and the like, to unforeseen accidents and surgery. (Speaking of veterinarians, is there one in your area who will treat wolfdogs? Many will not.) Add to that the cost of upgrading your existing fencing or building proper containment, which can range from a few hundred dollars for a small pen to over a thousand dollars for a large enclosure, and decide whether you can or want to make that kind of financial investment.

You are probably beginning to realize that there is a lot to consider before getting a wolfdog. I am not trying to paint a bleak picture or discourage you from sharing your life with a wolfdog if you are in the right situation to do so. My goal is to prevent wolfdogs from eventually ending up in rescue centers or euthanized. While many people feel that the challenges of living with these loving, intelligent companions are well worth the rewards, others become overwhelmed by those challenges and give up. Consider the information in this book, read everything you can get your hands on, talk to wolfdog owners and visit with their animals. Then and *only* then can you make a responsible, informed decision.

If you are a first-time potential wolfdog owner, consider getting a Malamute or Husky first. Those breeds share some of the same physical and behavioral traits as wolfdogs, and are a good way to evaluate whether you really want a dog who might be even more high maintenance. If you decide to get a wolfdog, choose a low content. If you have had wolfdogs before, consider adopting from a rescue group. Rescue centers across the country are overflowing with wolfdogs who would love to share your home. At the very least, do not purchase a wolfdog from a "backyard breeder" where temperament and other factors have not been carefully considered.

If you already share your life with wolfdogs be responsible, get them neutered, keep them properly contained, and educate others. And now, on to the specifics of living with wolfdogs!

Phantom gives Mom a kiss

Compatibility/Integrating Your Pack

Existing Pack Members

If you have pets other than canines, consider carefully before bringing a wolfdog into your home. A mature wolfdog could injure or even kill cats, birds, rabbits, or other small pets. A pup is less likely to do so than an adult, and if raised and socialized properly with other pets, might coexist peacefully; then again, he might not. I know of some low and mid content wolfdogs who are absolutely fine with the cats they were raised with—in fact, the cats run the house! I have also heard of a few high content wolfdogs who were raised with and live peaceably with cats, though it is not the norm. If you have small animals and have decided to add a wolfdog to your pack, please consider getting a low content. Although there are no guarantees, a low content wolfdog is generally less likely to have an extremely strong prey/chase drive than is a high content.

Gender Contenders

Unneutered male wolfdogs are more likely to fight with other males than are their neutered counterparts. However, neutering is no guarantee that two males will not fight. Males fight for rank in the pack order. Their fights are often very noisy, although there is normally not a great amount of damage once they settle who is in charge.

Fights between female wolfdogs, on the other hand, can be quiet and deadly. Female-female is the combination with the highest potential for violence. In a wolf pack, the alpha female is normally the only one to mate. She "suppresses" the other females in the pack so that they do not attempt to couple. If you have two females who are not spayed, you are setting yourself up for potential disaster when one comes into heat. *Think long and hard before bringing a female wolfdog into a home with another female.*

This is not to say that two female wolfdogs will absolutely not get along. But if you have the choice, why take a chance? A spayed/neutered female/male combination is your best bet.

> *Most dogs come into estrus twice a year. Wolves do so once a year, in Jan./Feb. Male wolves are only fertile late fall to early spring* (Sloan, Wolf Park). *Wolfdogs may cycle once or twice yearly. Gestation is 63 days for both wolves and dogs.*

Pleased to Meet You

How dogs are introduced can play a vital part in determining whether they will accept each other and be able to live together. While some dogs will simply not tolerate each other's presence from the start, most will engage in a getting-to-know-you ritual. This ritual involves checking each other out via scent and engaging in status-displaying physical postures involving tail carriage, ear position, body stance and more. If all goes well, one will offer a play invitation and the dogs will move on to friendly interactions.

Signs that things are not going well include stiff body postures, tails held high and wagging stiffly, curled lips, growling and other displays. If necessary, step in before things escalate into a fight. If you are not well versed in canine body language, having a professional trainer present to assess initial interactions can be extremely helpful. Although the dogs will make the ultimate determination, the following suggestions should help to stack the odds in favor of a smooth introduction.

Rag-Wipe Technique

The "rag-wipe technique" makes use of the fact that canines investigate each other via scent. When using this technique, take care when handling the dogs—if you detect any stiffening of the body, growling or other signs of discomfort, stop immediately. The following preparations are to be made before the dogs are introduced: Take a rag or towel and wipe it around the first dog's anal-genital region. That might sound odd, but that is where the scent glands are concentrated. Using the same rag, wipe it around the ruff (shoulder area) and rear of the second dog. Repeat the sequence by wiping that same rag around the second dog's anal-genital region and then around the first dog's ruff and rear. Now when the dogs sniff each other they will think, *Hey, there's something I like about this guy!* While the technique might not change matters if the dogs truly dislike each other, it is definitely helpful and cannot hurt to try.

Parallel Walking

Introducing new packmates on neutral territory is always best. In other words, do not bring your new wolfdog directly into your house or yard. If two vehicles are available, drive the dogs separately to meet at a local park. If that is not possible, stand with your new pack member at a distance from your house while a friend approaches with your dog. (The reason you are not holding your dog's leash is to prevent the chance that he might become protective over you.)

Do not let the dogs circle and sniff each other just yet. Instead, as your friend approaches, begin to walk in the same direction but at a distance from each other, with the dogs on the outside. Here is what parallel walking would look like, with both person/dog teams walking in the same direction:

> dog person   person dog

As you walk, if the dogs seem relaxed, move gradually closer together while maintaining the dogs' outside positions. Be sure to keep the mood light. Dogs sense when people are tense, and your muscle tension could easily transmit down the leash and cause your dog to become tense as well. Continue on your walk long enough to tire the dogs out a bit.

Assuming the dogs have walked together without showing signs of aggression, take them to a large, neutral, enclosed area such as a park. *Do not let the dogs off leash.* Leashes should be held to allow some slack (it should look like the leash is forming the letter J) while allowing the dogs to approach and sniff each other. Allowing slack is important, as many dogs become defensive on a tight leash. Even if the dogs seem to get along immediately, do not let them off-leash yet. Your new wolfdog is not sufficiently bonded with you or your other dog to reliably stay nearby. If all goes well at the neutral location, take both dogs home and walk them into the house or yard together.

Setup for Success

Whether your new pack member is a pup or an adult, be sure to lavish plenty of attention on your existing companion as well so he does not become resentful of the new addition. Supervise all interactions between the two, taking special care in the first few weeks. Step in and quietly break up any rough play that seems as though it might be escalating into aggression. Redirect the dogs to other activities, using an upbeat tone of voice and non-confrontational body language. Do not leave chew bones or toys lying around, since they could become catalysts for fights. At feeding time, place food bowls far enough apart that there will not be skirmishes. Supervise while the dogs eat and pick up bowls directly afterward. (Some dogs become possessive over an empty dish!) If necessary, feed your new pack member outside and your first one inside. If you see any signs that the dogs are not getting along, do not leave them alone together unsupervised, and seek professional help.

"Heeere, Kitty, Kitty..."

If you have a cat, use the rag-wipe technique before allowing actual physical introductions. Set up a barrier such as a high baby gate so that your wolfdog and your cat can meet safely. Baby gates are perfect for this purpose because they allow visual, olfactory and limited physical contact while keeping your fur-kids safely separated. Always supervise these getting-to-know-you sessions. If your wolfdog acts in a friendly manner, encourage him with lots of verbal praise. If you are not sure whether his behavior is friendly or is an indication of predation, have a behavior specialist do an evlaution or at the very least, keep the two separated until you are sure they will get along.

Assuming all goes well, until your cat and wolfdog become completely comfortable with each other, do not leave them alone unsupervised, even for a moment. And remember, baby gates will not present much of a challenge for an unsupervised wolfdog.

If your wolfdog shows signs of aggression or predation toward your cat, remove him from the area and, depending on how severe the display, reconsider whether it is a good match. If you are determined to keep both animals, consider how to safely manage the environment so the two never have access to each other.

Little Critters

Regarding birds, reptiles and other small pets, it is up to you to make sure they are kept safely out of range of your wolfdog. Keep them in a room with a door that can be locked; do not underestimate your wolfdog's ability to leap onto counters and to open doors that are not securely locked.

The bottom line is, until you are absolutely sure that your wolfdog and your other pets get along, *never leave them alone together unsupervised*. Be patient. With proper introductions and vigilance, your new member will soon feel like part of the pack.

Skittishness/Socialization

Sometimes wolfdog owners are surprised when their new furry family member seems to prefer hiding behind the couch to playing with them. "Is this normal?" they ask. The answer is yes. Wolves are naturally shy of people. In the wild, you are more likely to hear wolves howling than you are to see them. It stands to reason that many wolfdogs, especially high contents, are naturally skittish. Wolfdogs require extensive early socialization to help them to become comfortable around people, sounds, smells, places and other animals.

The optimum window for socialization in dogs is from four to twelve weeks of age. During that time, a genetically stable dog will accept exposure to most new stimuli without becoming fearful. That does not mean that pups older than twelve weeks cannot be introduced to new people and environments, but that the further the pup is from that age, the greater the chance of a fearful reaction. If your wolfdog is a pup, it is your job to make sure he receives early and ongoing socialization. If you do not continue to socialize your pup through adolesence into adulthood, he could regress and become desocialized. Desocialization is a common phenomenon among dogs who are moved from cities to rural areas where they no longer receive regular exposure to other dogs and people.

If you are taking in an adult animal, take heart. Even adult wolfdogs can be socialized. Given care and patience, many will adjust well to a new home environment. Although the following pages discuss socializing puppies, the same advice may be applied to adult wolfdogs; just take it one step at a time and move at the pace at which your wolfdog is comfortable.

Powder, a high content Arctic pup

Crates are Great

If you do not own a crate, purchase one immediately. (See *Housebreaking*). A crate is one of the best investments any puppy owner can make. Place a blanket or towel with your scent on it in the bottom of the crate, and prop the door open so it cannot swing shut by accident and scare your pup. Now your wolfdog has a safe place to retreat should he feel afraid. As an added bonus, the towel will get your pup accustomed to your scent in a non-threatening manner and help the bonding process.

Who's Afraid of the Big Bad Human?

Perhaps your pup is naturally outgoing, not afraid of you or anyone else. Great! But many are not this way. If your pup seems fearful, do *not* drag him out of his hiding place or force him to come to you or others. Let him approach in his own good time. If you feel he is comfortable enough that you can coax him to you, crouch down and turn your body slightly to the side so you are not facing him dead-on. Look down or away—a direct stare is a threat in the animal kingdom. You are communicating with your body language that you are not a threat. (With a fearful pup, you could even lie on the floor.) When you look at your pup do not stare, but instead, partially lower your lids and soften your gaze. If your pup seems comfortable and approaches, use slow movements to pet him on the chest or the side of the face.

> *Don't head-pat! When one dog puts a paw over the back or head of another dog, it is usually a gesture of dominance. The last thing a frightened pup needs is what it perceives as a gesture of dominance coming from a big, scary person.*

Hot Dogs are Your Friend

Diamonds may be a girl's best friend, but for wolfdog owners, it's definitely hot dogs. Hot dogs are an excellent way to lure your wolfdog to come near and to show him that close proximity to you yields good things. Break off a small piece of hot dog and gently toss it, low to the ground, a little bit in front of your wolfdog. Be sure the movement of your hand is small and slow, so as not to scare your pup. Let him eat the hot dog. Now that he is interested, with each successive piece, see if you can get him a bit closer. Take your time and do not push too far too fast. It might take a few sessions over time for him to take pieces from your hand. It takes time to build trust, so be patient. When your pup eventually takes the hot dogs from your hand, refrain from reaching for him. Pet him only when he seems comfortable.

Visitors or Predators?

Although you are probably eager to show off your new companion, do not overwhelm him with visits from large groups of people. Invite one or two visitors over at a time. Be aware that sunglasses and hats can be frightening to wolfdogs (and skittish dogs in general). From your wolfdog's point of view, it might seem as though these scary humans have weirdly shaped heads and giant black eyes! Have visitors remove these accessories before entering your home.

If your pup is very skittish, instruct visitors to ignore him completely. Explain that they are not to look at or talk to the pup, nor to make any startling sounds. If the pup approaches to sniff, they should remain motionless. In this way, your pup can get used to people at his own pace. Instruct visitors that once your pup approaches and seeks contact, they may use slow movements to pet him on the chest or the side of the face. If your pup is obviously comfortable with visitors, give them hot dogs to feed him. This will help him to associate visitors with good things.

Until your pup is fully vaccinated, use caution when choosing walking areas and playmates. Parvo and distemper, two potentially fatal canine diseases, could be contracted by a pup who walks where infected dogs have been. To avoid spreading disease, you and your visitors should step in a mixture of bleach and water before entering your home and wash hands before touching your pup. And never let your pup down on the floor in the veterinarian's office—after all, that is the most likely place for sick puppies to have been.

Tatanka, a low-to-mid content, takes refuge among the bunnies.

Other Pups, Human and Canine

Even if you do not have children of your own, it is important to socialize your wolfdog to kids. A wolfdog who has never been exposed to children could become suspicious and fearful of them as an adult. That situation is potentially dangerous, as it could lead to fear-based aggression toward children.

Do you have friends who have well-behaved kids? Invite them over. Supervise carefully when introducing children to your pup. Be sure they have been briefed on how to interact with the pup, stressing that they should not pull the pup's tail or ears, hit the pup or try to "ride" him. If you feel your pup might overwhelm the children by nipping or jumping, keep him on a leash for safety. And no matter how well-behaved the children or your pup might be, never leave them together unsupervised.

Do you have friends who have an outgoing dog? If so, assuming he is fully vaccinated and gets along well with puppies, invite them over. The dogs will probably jump at the chance to play together. In the process, the visiting dog is likely to engage happily with you as well. Your pup will see that you are not actually the Big Bad Human he feared you might be, and might become less fearful of you with the other dog present. *Note: Although your wolfdog should socialize with other canines, limit most of his early companionship to you and your family so that he bonds with you first and foremost.*

Well-adjusted adult dogs are excellent teachers of canine manners. Puppies, wolfdog or not, do not have much in the way of manners when they play with other dogs. They hurl themselves at other dogs, teeth and paws flying with wild abandon. Most adult dogs will put up with this behavior for a short time and then put the pup in his place. The adult might curl a lip, growl, or even threaten the pup to the extent that he rolls over on his back and submits. If that occurs, let it happen! As long as no one is getting hurt, the adult is teaching your pup a valuable lesson about interacting with other dogs. Letting your pup learn these lessons now can save you both a lot of grief later. Dogs who have never been taught how to play appropriately can be perceived as aggressive by other dogs, and fights can result.

The Sound of Music...and Other Scary Sounds

Everyday noises such as those made by the garbage disposal or vacuum cleaner can be frightening to a pup. To help him get used to these noises, stand with your pup far back from the appliance and have another person turn it on. If it has a volume control (e.g., a stereo), begin on low. If your pup startles, cowers or runs away, you have begun too close to the source of the sound.

Do not reinforce fearful behavior by cooing, "It's okay" or otherwise coddling your pup. If you want to reassure him say, "Don't be silly" in an off-hand, casual tone. Why does the first phrase and intonation reinforce fear while the latter has the opposite effect? Think of a child who falls and skins her knee. The parent who coos, "Oh honey, poor thing, let Mommy see" is sure to be rewarded with an outburst of tears. But the casual, "It's fine, nothing to worry about" is more likely to result in a child who wanders off to play, feeling safe and reassured. If the pack leader seems unconcerned, then obviously there is nothing to worry about!

Getting back to habituating to sounds...for sounds that are truly frightening to your wolfdog, pair the sound with treats. For example, if your wolfdog is afraid of the vacuum, stand with him in a room far from the vacuum, treats at the ready. Have someone turn on the vaccuum. As soon as you hear the sound, rapidly deliver treats, one after another. After a few seconds the vaccuum should stop, with you simultaneously stopping the treat delivery. Repeat. Keep sessions short. As your pup becomes more relaxed, move him gradually closer to the vacuum. You are using classical conditioning to create a good association between the vacuum and something your pup finds rewarding, so he will eventually come to have a positive emotional response to the sound of the vacuum. Keep classical conditioning in mind so you can apply it when necessary. This desensitization process might take days or weeks; be patient. Classical conditioning may also be used if your wolfdog is afraid of movements or objects (although some motion sensitivity might be genetic). Start slowly and build gradually; stop and go back a step or two if your pup seems uncomfortable.

When you are out in public and something scares your pup, he might run behind your legs as if to say, "Mom, hide me!" Again, do not pick him up, pet or coo, and do not force him to approach the thing that is scaring him. Instead, just stand there as though there is nothing to worry about. Breathe and try to relax. You might even hum or sing a silly song under your breath. Remember, dogs pick up on our emotional state and tension can easily be transmitted down the leash. Wolfdogs, being the sensitive creatures that they are, are certainly no exception.

You've Got the Touch

As your pup becomes more comfortable around you, it is important that you get him accustomed to physical touch. Gently touch his paws, softly rubbing and spreading toe pads; check his ears, gently looking inside; open his mouth, hold for a second, then close; pull lips back to inspect the gums. If you intend to brush your wolfdog's teeth, start by putting a bit of doggie toothpaste on your finger and briefly massaging his gums. Don't forget the praise!

Another type of handling to get your pup used to is being restrained. Ask your veterinarian's office to show you the method they use to restrain dogs for exams or vaccinations, then go home and practice with your pup. Another exercise you can do at home will get your pup accustomed to being held. Sit on the floor and cradle him on his back in your lap. If he squirms do not reprimand in any way; just hold him firmly. As soon as he relaxes say, "Good boy!" and let him go. He will soon learn that relaxing and allowing himself to be held is the way to get what he wants.

Massage is another useful form of handling. There are books and videos that teach specific methods of canine massage (TTouch is a popular one), but you can also do intuitive massage without instruction. Choose a time when your wolfdog is pleasantly worn out. Begin by speaking gently as you pet him in long, even strokes from shoulders to rear. As he relaxes, move into massage. The motions used to massage a dog are the same as for a person. Use small, circular motions or deeper kneading, depending on the area of the body. Do not massage over bone. Large muscles may be kneaded more deeply, but be aware of any areas on your wolfdog's body where he seems sensitive and adjust your pressure accordingly. You might have to work up to being able to massage certain areas, so be patient. Making massage a daily habit can alert you to lumps or other abnormalities early on, and provides a pleasant bonding experience for you both.

Meanwhile, Back at the Rescue...

Back to our skittish friends... I would like to share a bit of my own experience with adult wolfdogs living in a rescue center. It might help with your wolfdog, especially if you have rescued an adult. Most adults who come to the rescue are shy at first, some extremely so. Although there have been a few who have never come around, over time, most have. The key is patience. I am always careful to give a new wolf or wolfdog their own space. I would not, for example, enter a pen and proceed directly to the back where the wolfdog is cringing. Instead, keeping my movements slow, voice soft and eyes averted, I sit towards the front of the pen, near one of the sides. I want to give the wolfdog plenty of room to get past me. I sit with my body turned slightly away, indicating that I am not a threat. And although I speak quietly, I do not look at the wolfdog. I will, however, keep him within my peripheral vision—a good habit to get into, especially when working with adult rescues, for safety reasons.

Some wolfdogs will, after a few moments, approach to sniff my back or hair. Some will even sniff my underarms—it can be hard not to laugh! I remain motionless as the wolfdog investigates, though I will continue to talk in a soothing manner. When I feel he is comfortable enough, I might slowly move a hand an inch or two toward him (curled into a fist, palm down, usually on the ground) to sniff. When it gets to the point where I can pet him (which could be minutes or months depending on the animal), I do so on the chest and the sides of the face. I want to win his confidence, not show him who is boss.

Another tactic I have used with success makes use of the wolfdog's instinct to investigate scent. After sitting in one spot for a while, I will slowly rise and move to another spot in the pen, far enough away so the wolfdog can comfortably approach the first spot. This investigation is usually immediate, and provides a non-threatening way to check out my scent without having to actually approach me. I have observed many wolves and wolfdogs become more comfortable after this ritual. In your living room, this would translate to your sitting on a sofa or chair and then moving to another piece of furniture, giving your wolfdog enough space to approach the first. If you have a wolfdog who is so shy he hides behind furniture, try placing a T-shirt, sweatshirt, or towel with your scent on it in the areas where he likes to hang out. Just spending time in the same room, talking in a soothing voice, moving slowly, perhaps reading from a book (anything but *Little Red Riding Hood*!) and being patient should eventually yield results. See the *Resources* section for *Calming Signals*, a helpful book about recognizing canine stress signals and how we can use our body language to help put dogs at ease.

Hang in there. I know how frustrating it can be. There will be times when you wonder what you have gotten yourself into, having an animal that will not come near you. But the first time your wolfdog approaches and gives you a big, slurpy kiss on the face, you will know it was all worthwhile.

Housebreaking

Whether your wolfdog is an adult or a pup, if you expect him to spend time in the house (and you should), he must be reliably housebroken. Many people believe that wolfdogs cannot be housebroken. Untrue! What *is* true is that the higher the wolf content, the higher the chances that housebreaking will take more time and effort. Whatever the content of your wolfdog, crate training is an excellent way to accomplish the task. Crating works because of the canine instinct not to soil in one's own area. In your home, the crate will become your wolfdog's "den," a safe place where he can sleep, relax, and take refuge if he is feeling ill or afraid. A crate also comes in handy when you need to transport your wolfdog, to limit his movement after surgery or injury, or to contain him in an emergency situation.

What Size and Type of Crate Will I Need?

As you will find at your local pet supply store, there are many brands of crates, but only two main types. The first type consists of a hard plastic top and bottom that snap together, with open slats on the sides for ventilation and a metal grille door. The second type is metal. It looks more like a cage, and folds down into a convenient suitcase-like shape for carrying. Some owners prefer the metal type for heavy-coated dogs, as the open design allows for greater ventilation. I personally prefer the plastic type even for heavy-coated dogs, as it gives more of an enclosed, safe feeling. If you want to create more of a "den" effect in a metal crate, place a blanket or towel over the top and two sides.

A new, quality crate for a medium-to-large sized wolfdog will cost approximately fifty to one hundred dollars. While that might sound expensive, it is money well spent. A damaged carpet alone would cost more to replace!

The crate should be just big enough for your wolfdog to stand up and turn around. If you have a pup, do not buy a huge crate for him to grow into. Having all that spare room will defeat the purpose. You could purchase a puppy-sized crate now and a larger one as he grows. Or, purchase a large metal crate that comes with dividers so the space can be made smaller at first and then expanded as needed.

How Do I Introduce my Wolfdog to the Crate?

The sooner you start crate training the better. Place a blanket or old sweatshirt with your scent on it in the bottom of the crate. This will not only make your wolfdog more comfortable, but will assist in the bonding process. Place the crate in a high-traffic area of your home, such as the living room. Leave plenty of time for your wolfdog to explore the crate, as opposed to getting him familiar with it right before bedtime.

Be sure the door is propped open so as not to swing shut by accident and scare your pup. Do not force him into the crate—doing so could form an unpleasant association and make things difficult for both of you down the road. Instead, toss a treat toward the back of the crate and say, "Go to bed" in a soft, pleasant voice. (This verbal cue will eventually become associated with entering the crate, which is helpful at bedtime and when traveling.) If your pup enters, allow him to eat the treat and exit the crate. If he does not seem to see the treat, try removing the blanket and making sure that when you toss, the treat hits the back of the crate and makes a sound. *(Note: Although we are using a puppy as an example, this method works for adult wolfdogs as well.)*

Some pups will be too fearful to enter the crate, even with tempting food morsels inside. In that case, go slow. Place a food treat right on the crate's entry lip and let your pup take it. Gradually place treats further and further inside. Be sure not to hover near the crate, as a wary canine might view the whole setup as a trap! It might be necessary for you to take a few steps away from the crate and ignore your pup altogether.

Once your pup is comfortable following a treat into the crate and you have repeated the sequence ten to fifteen times, sit back and wait. Most pups will either enter the crate again, or at least step toward or look at the crate. If your pup does any of those things, toss a treat inside. Whereas before you were *luring* your pup into the crate with the tossed treat, now you are *rewarding* him for any interaction with the crate. You will find that if you take it in small increments, your wolfdog will soon be standing or lying in the crate waiting to receive treats. After rewarding your pup a few times for being inside the crate, shut the door with one hand and rapidly feed a few treats through the metal grille door with the other. Immediately open the door and let your pup out. (To view a DVD showing this sequence, see *Resources* for *Train Your Dog: the Positive, Gentle Method.*) Repeat, gradually building up to having the door closed for longer periods. Once your wolfdog seems comfortable with being closed inside, give chew bones and meals in the crate now and then to create further good associations with being crated.

Once your pup is used to the crate, begin crating him overnight. Some owners think, *I don't want the crate in my bedroom. I'll get woken up during the night.* Well yes, you will. But that is because your pup is just a baby, and he cannot be expected to hold it all night. If he is crated in your room, you will hear a frantic whining if he needs to urinate. Carry him to the appropriate spot, let him urinate, praise and return him to the crate. If he were in another room you might not hear his fervent pleas, which might force him to urinate in the crate; that would defeat the whole purpose of crate training. Besides, allowing your pup to sleep in the same room with you is helpful to the bonding process. After all, he is a member of your pack!

If you take your pup out to potty during the night, once he has finished, put him back in the crate and go back to sleep. Do not get in the habit of playing with him in the middle of the night. It is difficult to get a wolfdog who thinks that 2 a.m. is playtime to potty and then return to a crate without a fuss!

While you will come to know the frantic *I have to go right now!* whine, it is also perfectly normal for any dog to whine, bark or even throw tantrums the first night in a crate, especially when he is first placed inside. Do *not* reward this behavior by petting, whispering soothing words, or worst of all, letting him out. If you do, he will learn in short order what works and will continue those tactics. Instead, try to ignore it. Wait it out. If you can catch him being silent for five seconds say, "Good boy" in a calm voice or pet him through the crate door briefly. If you cannot get even five seconds of silence say, "Quiet" in a stern voice, then tap the top of the crate. Just avoid getting into an endless cycle of him crying and you responding with "Quiet," as any type of attention could be perceived as a reward. Most pups will soon feel comfortable sleeping in the crate and will only whine when they truly need to urinate.

Potty on Cue

It is helpful to instill a verbal cue such as "Hurry up" or "Go potty" to instruct your pup to urinate on command. First thing in the morning, open the crate door and carry or quick-walk your pup to the designated elimination area. He will probably be ready to urinate almost immediately. When you see him circle, sniff or give other signs that he is about to urinate, utter your cue words in a soft voice so as not to startle him out of what he is doing. Once he has finished, offer effusive praise. If you want to reward with a treat, offer it immediately after he has finished eliminating. (If you give the treat after returning indoors, you are rewarding him for coming indoors.) Pair the cue words with the pre-urination ritual throughout the day. Within a few weeks, you should be able to cue your pup to urinate. This type of control comes in handy, especially when traveling with your pup or in inclement weather.

Supervision

During the day, supervision is an absolute must. *Your pup should not be out of your sight unsupervised for even a few seconds.* There are a few ways to accomplish this goal. One is to attach a leash to your belt or a loop on the waist of your pants, using a double-sided clip. Your pup will be forced to go where you go, which is good not only for supervision, but for leadership. (And you thought Follow the Leader was just a kids' game.)

Another way to keep your pup out of trouble is to tether him. Wrap a leash around the leg of a sturdy piece of furniture, such as a couch. Slip the clip through the loop and attach it to your pup's collar. The idea is that when you plan to be in one room for a while, although your attention might wander, your pup cannot. It is important to introduce your pup to the tether in a way that will create a good association. Tether him with a great chew bone or treats, or sit and pet him. Do not leave your pup tethered unsupervised. If your pup is the type to chew through a leash, use a short, steel-coated cable tether instead. (See *Resources*.) If you need to shower or be otherwise indisposed and you do not want your pup in the room with you, place him in his crate or in a room with a baby gate across it until you can once again supervise.

If your pup is not leashed or tethered and you catch him starting to squat or to circle and sniff, startle him with a sharp sound such as a hand-clap or a loud verbal "Eh-eh!" then quickly take him to the proper elimination spot. Don't forget the praise if he elminates. If, on the other hand, you walk into a room to find an accident that has already happened, consider it your own mistake and clean it up quietly. You should have been supervising! Besides, canines do not associate a correction with the offensive act if the correction comes more than a few seconds after the fact.

Use a cleaning product that removes not only the stain, but the odor; otherwise your pup might be tempted to urinate over the same spot again. *Nature's Miracle*™ has been a favorite of dog owners for years. Anothr product called *Anti-Icky-Poo*™ contains genetically altered bacteria that actually "eat" the urine and fecal matter, leaving carpets stain and odor free. (See *Resources*.)

Take your wolfdog out to eliminate upon first waking, after naps, after meals, after playtime and before bed. A young pup should be taken out at least once every hour. Feed at roughly the same times each day. Keeping to a consistent feeding and elimination schedule is an important part of the housebreaking process.

If you must leave the house for short periods, you may leave your wolfdog crated—but never for more than three to four hours at a time, and only for the length of time he can hold his urine. Leave a favorite safe toy or chew bone in the crate with him to alleviate boredom. Until he is reliably housebroken, confining your pup to the crate while you are gone will help to prevent "accidents" and will also prevent inappropriate chewing and other destruction. If you must be away for longer periods, place your pup in a laundry room or kitchen area with a baby gate across the doorway. Place his crate (with open door) at one end of the area and a puppy pad or newspaper at the opposite end to give him a place to eliminate.

Crate training will help immensely with housebreaking, but it is important to remember that your own consistency in supervision is crucial. The more you are there to give well-timed interruptions and praise, the faster your pup will learn. Some wolfdogs are housebroken within seven to ten days, while others take weeks or even months.

Once your wolfdog is housebroken, you can still use the crate for confinement when necessary. Even with the door open, many wolfdogs choose to sleep, hang out, and take refuge in their crates. Crate training is well worth the time and effort, and will give your wolfdog a permanent place of safety and comfort.

"Hey, who's got the remote?"

Misha and Jack, two very content mid-contents

Containment for your Canine Houdini

Wolfdogs are notorious escape artists. They can leap tall fences in a single bound or dig under in minutes flat. They are also extremely intelligent problem-solvers. Watching you fiddle with a gate latch once might be all it takes for a wolfdog to understand how to open it the next time. Amazing, isn't it? But not to worry. No matter how your back yard is configured, there *is* a way to keep your wolfdog safely contained.

Once a wolfdog escapes and has been rewarded with the joys of roaming the neighborhood, he is more likely to persist in trying to escape again. Building adequate containment the first time around is crucial. There are three ways out of a fenced yard (other than a gate that has been left open): chewing through, jumping over and digging under. Following are solutions to each.

Break on Through

Chewing through does not happen with the frequency of digging under or jumping over, but it is not uncommon, especially among very high content wolfdogs. If your wolfdog chews through eleven-gauge (standard) chain link, if possible, replace it with nine-gauge, which is thicker and stronger. If you have wooden fencing, check the slats and replace or reinforce those that are weak or worn. If replacing your fencing is not possible, one option is to build an escape-proof pen. (See page 55.) Another is to add "hot wire" to your existing fence. Hot wire will be discussed later in this chapter.

Over and Out

In many cases, over-the-top escapes can be thwarted by adding lean-ins. Lean-ins are metal (or wooden) arms that are bent at a 45-degree angle. Once they have been attached at intervals to the top of fencing, wire is stretched between them. Lean-ins are commonly used at zoos to give animals the illusion that the fencing is impossible to scale.

Lean-in arms can be purchased from a building materials supplier. Some lean-ins come already attached to metal caps that in turn attach to the top of chain link posts. Others are sold individually. Individual arms can be attached by drilling into chain link posts. Once the arms are attached, stretch chicken wire or other non-barbed wire tautly between them and secure with hog rings or wire. Never use barbed wire between the arms, as your wolfdog might try to clear the fence anyway and could be seriously injured.

Lean-ins can be used with wooden fencing as well. Either plant wooden posts at intervals and attach the lean-in arms to the tops of the posts, or drill holes in your existing fence to attach the arms. Another option to bolster wooden fencing is to string hot wire. (See diagram next page.)

Simply Shocking!

The thought of any type of animal being shocked is extremely unpleasant. However, the thought of your wolfdog escaping and being lost, confiscated by animal control, or hit by a car is distinctly less pleasant. For that reason, many wolfdog owners use hot wire to prevent dig-outs and over-the-top escapes. Hot wire is an electrified wire or wires that deliver a shock on contact. It should always be used in conjunction with existing fencing rather than as a primary means of containment.

Regardless of how hot wire is configured, there are four basic components to the system: the wire itself, the insulator clamps it must be seated on, the unit that plugs into an electrical outlet (battery-powered chargers are also available), and the ground pole, which is a metal pole that is sunk into the ground and attaches to the unit by a separate wire.

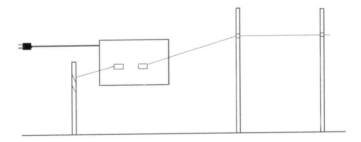

Steel wire is cheap but rusts, which would disrupt the flow of electricity; aluminum is a bit more expensive but worth it. Using one continuous length of wire is best but if necessary, the wire can easily be spliced by wrapping one loose end around the other. There are two common levels of voltage. A standard charger will deliver a shock that is slightly stronger than what you would receive from shuffling your feet on carpeting and then touching metal. A "cattle grade" charger will deliver a stronger shock. While you should use the lowest level that works, some wolfdog owners find it necessary to use cattle grade chargers to keep their extremely persistent wolfdogs contained. Take care with exposed wires and poles so that no one will trip on them and dog collars will not catch on them. Chargers, wire, ground poles and insulated clamps can be purchased at hardware stores.

Though adequate containment is a must, it is hoped that when you are at home your wolfdog will be in the house with you, or at least free to run in your yard with supervision. Providing companionship and exercise are an important part of successful containment. A wolfdog who is constantly left alone will be a lonely, unhappy animal who is likely to try to escape. And who could blame him?

Configurations

For a large area such as a back yard, hot wire should be strung around the perimeter at the top of existing chain link or wooden fencing. The wire must be strung through insulated clamps that should first be attached to posts just above the top of your fence. For example, you could attach the clamps to short wooden garden stakes, then attach those stakes at intervals to the top of your fence. A wolfdog who jumps and is not touching the ground nor the fence when he makes contact with the wire, however, is not grounded and would not receive a shock. It is necessary to run two strands of wire, one approximately ¼-½ inch under the other, so that contact is made with both wires and a shock is delivered.

Dig This

Hot wire can also be used to prevent digging out, and to keep your wolfdog from destroying flower beds around the perimeter of your yard. While you can piece together a system as previously described, there is also a ready-made, complete system available. Sold under the brand name Fido Shock™, this surprisingly affordable package includes plastic stakes, wire, clamps, electrical unit and ground pole.

The stakes should be planted a yard or so apart, about two feet in all the way around your fence line. The clamps slip easily into pre-drilled holes in the stakes. The wire is then threaded through the clamps and attached to the electrical unit, which is plugged into an outlet on your house. The ground pole is planted in the ground and attached to the electrical unit with a separate wire. Plug it in and you're ready to go!

The wire should be at your wolfdog's chest level so that he will be less likely to go under or over it. Some owners prefer to use two wires, one at knee level and one at chest level. If your wolfdog touches the wire, a mild electrical shock will be delivered. Don't worry, it is nothing that will fling him across the yard or injure him in any way. It *will* likely deter him from going near it again. My own two fur-kids had very different reactions to the hot wire: Soko, who is very sensitive, got shocked once and refused to enter the yard for a few days; she was convinced there was a monster out there. Mojo, on the other hand, touched it with his nose, gave a canine version of a Homer Simpson "D'oh!" and then immediately did it two more times. I love that boy, but sometimes he is not the brightest bulb in the string... They both have a total respect for that wire now, and what they do not know is that Mom unplugged the system months ago. The nice thing about this pre-packaged system (besides the low cost), is that it is extremely easy to install and covers a large area. Just be sure to keep leaves and debris away from the wire to prevent short circuiting the system, and check periodically to see that the system is operating (testers are available at pet supply and hardware stores).

An alternate method of preventing dig-outs involves attaching a skirting of sturdy wire to the bottom of your fence. This method is better suited for use with chain link fencing than wooden fencing. You will need a roll of chain link or galvanized wire, a small spool of wire, wire-cutters, and if you are using rolled chain link, a strong pair of bolt-cutters. Galvanized wire usually measures approximately four feet across and is sometimes sold under the name "garden fencing." Some galvanized wire has large rectangular openings; some looks like graph paper would if it were made of metal. Galvanized wire is not as strong as chain link, but is sturdier than chicken wire.

Lay the galvanized wire or chain link skirting out along the bottom of your fence. Attach it to the fence using the spooled wire (cut lengths of five feet or less for easy handling) by threading the wire through a bottom diamond in the chain link (push it through forwards, away from you), then looping it around the bottom rail of the fence, up through the skirting and back over again. (See diagram p.55.) Skipping every other diamond, continue as though you are sewing two pieces of fabric together. A word of caution about working with wire—*wear gloves*! That might seem like common sense but it is worth repeating; bare hands blister and are easily sliced. Yours truly found this out the hard way—don't you do it. Once you have finished sewing the skirting into place, shovel dirt over the top and pack it down. You should now have a barrier that will prevent even a wolfdog from digging out.

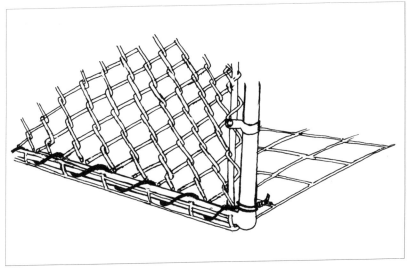

Garden fencing wired to upright chain link
panel using the "sewing technique"

Pen Pals

Building an escape-proof pen takes a bit of time and effort, but it is worthwhile for a few reasons. First, you will have peace of mind knowing that your wolfdogs are safely contained. Second, a pen will stop your wolfdogs from digging up your yard and wreaking havoc on anything they can get their big paws on while you are gone. And last but not least, since your pen will be built at least two feet in from your perimeter fence, there will be no chance of children teasing your wolfdog through the fence and possibly being bitten, or someone poisoning or stealing your beloved companion.

An even better option than simply building your pen away from your yard fence is to build a perimeter fence two feet out around your pen. But for now, let's get your main pen built. Don't be intimidated by the construction aspects of this project. It is actually simple, although you will probably need a helper to maneuver the chain link panels into place and to help with the top. Just remember, you only have to build it once, and it's worth it. *Proper containment can save your wolfdog's life.*

Most dog pens are four-sided chain-link enclosures. Your pen, however, will be six-sided, as containing a wolfdog requires a top and a dig-proof bottom. Measure the area to determine what length chain link panels to use. The larger you can build the pen, the better. Do it right the first time—tearing down and expanding is no fun, believe me. If you plan to make the pen twelve feet wide, either six- or twelve-foot panels will work. Regardless of the width you choose, the panels should be at least six feet high and made of at least eleven-gauge chain link. (Nine-gauge is stronger; the lower the number, the stronger the chain link.) You could also use chain link panels across the top. Chain link panels can be purchased from a building materials supplier. You might also find used panels or even a second-hand dog run in your local newspaper classifieds.

Choose a flat area, set back at least two feet from your perimeter fence. Set up the four side panels first and secure them to each other using clamps and bolts. Try to keep the panels lined up and flush, and be sure all nuts are tightened. Now we move on to the dig-proof bottom. If you own your home and can build something permanent, concrete can be poured. If you are lucky enough to already have a concreted patio area, you might consider using part of that as the floor pad. If concrete flooring is not possible, read on.

The best way to dig-proof the bottom of your pen is with rolled chain link. Chain link rolls are normally four feet wide. Lay the chain link out lengthwise in side-by-side strips until the entire floor is covered. For example, if your pen is twelve feet wide, lay three four-foot-wide lengths side by side. Attach the outer sides of the strips to the bottom rails of the chain link panels using the sewing technique. Then attach the strips to each other using hog rings, or sew them together with the spooled wire. Once the chain link strips are secure, cover them with dirt. Some wolfdog owners prefer to add pea pea gravel, which is small, rounded stones that help to keep the dust down and the pen clean. If you use pea gravel, place bricks or large rocks around the inside perimeter of the pen first so the gravel does not spill out the sides. If you really want to go wild, instead of pea gravel, add paver stones. Pavers are flat, usually square, cement stones that can be found at building supply stores. If you opt for paver stones, a thin layer of sand poured first will keep the pavers flat and even.

Paver stones help to keep this pen clean and attractive

Now that the bottom is in place, let's move on to the top. If you are using chain link panels, simply lay them across the top of the pen and wire them down securely. If your pen is too wide to use top panels, or you prefer not to use them, use rolled chain link instead. Because of the weight of the material, it may be necessary to lay metal support bars or cables across the top first. Lay the chain link out in side by side strips then wire it down, as you did with the bottom. Once the panels or strips are attached, you could lay a garage door or other heavy wooden slab (coated with weather-sealant) over a portion of the top and secure by drilling holes and wiring it down. This top will provide shelter from the elements and a shaded area as well. *Caution: Garage doors are extremely heavy; you will need help hoisting them up.* Shade cloth is a lighter, easier alternative that can be easily attached. While it will not provide shelter from rain, it will help to keep your wolfdog cool on hot days.

Finish by placing a dog house inside. If your flooring is concrete, add a wooden platform on which your wolfdog can rest—lying on concrete constantly can cause skin and skeletal problems. Make the pen interesting by adding platforms to climb on, tunnels to crawl through, etcetera. (For more enrichment ideas see *Wolfdogs A-Z*.) Be sure your gate latch is secure. Add a chain and padlock and *viola' !* You now have a pen that should keep Timber safe and your neighbors happy.

~ * ~ * ~ * ~ * ~ * ~ * ~ * ~ *

So you see, there are a variety of options for containing your wolfdog. It *can* be done, so there is no excuse for your wolfdog to ever escape from your yard. Remember, if he does get out, there is a chance that you might not get him back. Proper enclosures take money, time and effort to build, but the safety of your wolfdog and your own peace of mind is surely worth it.

Spirit, Nashaka and Lobo - mid contents

Nicole and Spirit

Training

Can Wolfdogs be Trained?

Whether or not wolfdogs can be trained is a topic that tends to generate controversy. Even if owners agree that they *can* be trained, there is often disagreement as to *how* to train and to what extent one can expect reliability. Most people consider a well-trained canine to be one who responds to basic commands such as "sit" or "come." While the basics are important, there is more to it. A well-trained canine has manners. He does not jump on visitors or counter-tops, does not nip, and takes offered food gently. He is attentive and will respond to commands regardless of environment or distractions. That level of success in training is the result of ongoing communication between dog and trainer, as opposed to a set number of training sessions. Clear and ongoing communication is extremely important when training wolfdogs.

Canine intelligence levels vary from breed to breed and from dog to dog. Wolfdogs are typically a mix of wolf and either Malamute, Husky or German Shepherd. Sometimes behaviors that are attributed to an animal being part wolf are actually characteristic of the dog breed in the mix. For example, a wolfdog who is mostly German Shepherd might be perceived as protective. Although the dog might indeed display that trait, it is typical of German Shepherds, not wolves. Wolves and high content wolfdogs are more likely to run away from a threat than they are to defend their owners.

Pure wolves are extremely intelligent and will perform an action if they feel it benefits them, i.e., there is a reward. At Wolf Park, a well-known educational and research facility in Indiana, an adult male wolf named Socrates was taught, by using rewards, to jump through a hoop. Many low and some mid content wolfdogs can be trained as easily as dogs; some take longer and require more patience and consistency. A pure wolf or high content wolfdog will probably not comply with certain commands with the same degree of reliability as a dog. For example, it is much easier to teach the average dog to "leave it"—back away from an object or possession—than it is to get a wolf to comply. (Since wolves seem to live by the rule "what's theirs is theirs and what's yours is theirs," making a trade for something the wolf perceives to be of higher value works better and avoids a nasty confrontation.) A pure wolf or high content wolfdog is also less likely to have a perfectly reliable recall (come when called) than is a dog. Again, that is not to imply that wolfdogs cannot be trained to come when called or to perform behaviors on cue, but that the higher the wolf content, the greater the possibility that the behavior will not be as reliable as that of a dog.

Socrates demonstrates the power of lure/reward

The worst thing a wolfdog owner can do in regard to training is to make excuses for his animal based on wolf content. I have heard people say, "He's part wolf—of *course* he can't be trained." Untrue! One woman I knew bought a beautiful, black, golden-eyed wolfdog from a breeder. The breeder told her it would be impossible to housebreak or obedience train the low content wolfdog "because it's part wolf." The woman, not knowing any better, kept poor Thunder outside twenty-four hours a day and never attempted to train him. Naturally, without attention or companionship, Thunder became bored, destructive and desocialized. The woman eventually gave up on this "unmanageable beast." Fortunately, I was able to find Thunder a new home with an owner who knew better. He became housebroken, learned obedience and manners, and lived a long, happy life with his new family.

"It is not as important to train a wolfdog, it is more important to train them. Will it be more work than with most dogs? Generally, yes. Will the results be as good or as reliable with the same amount of time and effort as with a dog? Generally, no. However, an untrained, unworked with canine is a neglected canine. Wolves are more intelligent and investigative than most dogs and this can lead to easier boredom and a number of behavior problems including aggression. So more work is not only necessary, but the need is far greater in the wolfdog."

- Monty Sloan,
Wolf Behavior Specialist, Wolf Park

Accentuate the Positive

Regardless of the amount of wolf in your wolfdog, the old, harsh, choke-chain-jerking method of training is not a wise choice. In the last twenty years, there has been a movement toward professional trainers employing positive training methods, with excellent results. Karen Pryor, author of *Don't Shoot the Dog,* made a splash when she shaped the behavior of dolphins by using rewards. Paul Owens' book *The Dog Whisperer* not only offered excellent training advice, but taught about compassion and non-violence when relating to animals. Dr. Ian Dunbar's *Sirius Training* changed the way owners thought about teaching their dogs, using lure-reward and positive reinforcement methods. Dr. Dunbar also founded the APDT (Association of Pet Dog Trainers), an excellent organization that educates trainers and the public alike and has greatly helped in the advancement of the positive training movement. (See *Resources* for these books and APDT contact information.)

The following example illustrates the differences between force-based and non-coercive methods in teaching a dog to walk by his owner's side. Method One: dog, wearing choke chain, sits by owner's side. Owner says, "Heel!" and begins to walk. Each time dog gets ahead of owner, she jerks chain to deliver physical correction. (This would be like you being expected to perform a ballroom dance you have not been taught, and each time you make a mistake, your partner stomps on your foot!) Method Two: dog, wearing flat buckle collar, sits by owner's side. Owner has treats. Owner says, "Let's go!" and begins to walk, immediately delivering treat to dog for being in correct position. As owner proceeds, she continues to reward dog for being in correct position. If dog gets out ahead, owner gently turns and walks in opposite direction until dog is in proper position again, then rewards.

Method one punishes the dog in a harsh physical manner for not obeying; but the dog was never taught what was expected in the first place! Method two teaches the dog step by step what is expected, and rewards him for performing correctly. (Of course, with either method these are only the initial steps.) Which way would *you* prefer to be taught?

Not only are positive methods kinder and more fun for dog and owner, they are much safer when dealing with wolfdogs. While a dog who feels threatened might cower or snap when feeling threatened, a wolfdog is likely to give the trainer who caused that fear an instant, unforgettable lesson about why using force and coercion is a bad idea. If the last time you trained a dog or read a book about training involved harsh, coercive methods, re-educate yourself before attempting to train your wolfdog. There are many useful books and resources available, including my book *Wolfdogs A-Z: Behavior, Training and More* and the DVD *Train Your Dog: The Positive, Gentle Method.* (See *Resources.*) For a referral to a trainer in your area, see www.apdt.com.

Another way to train your wolfdog is to take him to a group class. A group class provides not only a learning experience, but the opportunity for your wolfdog to become comfortable around other dogs. Socialization is extremely important for canines, wolfdog or not; without it, your wolfdog could develop fear-aggression issues toward other dogs as he matures. Many low and mid content wolfdogs have passed obedience class with flying colors.

Training will help to reinforce your own status as pack leader and will gradually mold your wolfdog into a good house-mate. Just don't get so wrapped up in what you are doing that training becomes a grim task. Training sessions should be fun, happy experiences for you both.

"My, what big teeth you have!"

Mouthiness

Bite Inhibition

Because canines do not have opposable thumbs, they use their mouths to play, explore the world and defend themselves. Mouthing and nipping are normal canine behaviors. (Mouthing is more of a gentle, ongoing motion while nipping is sharper and faster.) When pups wrestle and play, if one bites down too hard, the offended pup yelps. That feedback is how pups begin to learn *bite inhibition*, to control jaw pressure. If you do not continue the lesson, you could end up as a very unhappy human pin-cushion. Teaching a pup bite inhibition is infinitely preferable to convincing a 120-pound adult with well-developed canines not to use you as a chew toy. This is not to say that adult wolfdogs cannot learn proper oral etiquette—they can, and it is up to us to teach. Teaching bite inhibition is especially important in the case of wolfdogs. If your wolfdog delivers a nip to a stranger (especially a child) that is interpreted as a bite, you could be sued and your wolfdog could be euthanized by court order.

Stack the odds in your favor by providing your pup with plenty of exercise and proper chew toys. The more energy he expends on those things, the less he will have left for nipping. Be careful not to inadvertently reward nipping by responding with play or attention; that would only teach your pup to nip you in order to solicit those things. And always be consistent in your definition of what is allowed and what is not.

Regardless of which technique you use, correct your pup first for hard nips or mouthing only. As he learns, correct for progressively lighter interactions, until he has learned not to put his teeth on people altogether. As with any training, consistency is key. But if one method does not yield noticeable improvement after you have tried it for a week, move on to another.

Instructions for Human Pups

Children are often the target of puppy nipping. Kids respond by flailing their arms, screaming or running, all of which is very exciting to a pup! Teach your kids that when the pup nips, to "be a tree." Being a tree means folding the arms with hands tucked under the armpits, and standing still. This manuever often has the immediate effect of the pup wandering off in search of a more exciting playmate. Of course, your child should not be expected to stand there if the pup continues to nip. In that case, an adult should step in and remove the pup from the area or redirect him to another activity or chew toy.

Children should be taught not only what to do when the pup nips, but how to avoid encouraging nipping in the first place. Children often pet pups palm-down over the head, and some pull their hands back at the last moment for fear of being nipped. Pups often respond by raising their head and nipping at the approaching hand. Teach kids to pet the pup on the chest or the side of the face instead, using slow, gentle movements. Do not allow children to pick up the pup unless they are sitting on the floor. Show them how to support the pup's stomach and chest, and teach that a pup should never be lifted by the shoulders, as it could result in joint dislocation or torn soft tissue.

Try to arrange to have child-pup interaction time when both parties are pleasantly tired out. Teach kids to pet as the pup chews on a bone or toy (assuming there are no resource guarding issues), and to never to attempt to take the object away. Your child can also hold a toy when approaching your pup so that if the pup starts to nip, the toy can be placed in his mouth. Teach your children that they are never to physically correct the pup for nipping or anything else. If you are not in the room and the dog does something "bad," they should call for help immediately.

The Lick-Lick Trick

Whenever you want your pup to stop doing something, think about what he could do instead. Instead of nipping, how about licking? The "lick-lick trick" teaches your pup to lick on request and is fun for kids as well. You try it first: Spread a thin coat of peanut butter on the back of your hand. Position the hand with closed fist just under your pup's nose. Say, "lick-lick" (or if you prefer, "kisses") in a high, happy voice, praising as he licks. After a few seconds, remove the hand and re-present it, repeating the verbal cue. Do a few repetitions, then help your kids to practice. After a few days of practice, test whether your pup understands the cue by presenting your closed fist sans peanut butter and asking him to lick. If he does, great! If not, practice a bit more and try again.

Another way to help your pup to associate the verbal cue with licking is to give the cue each time he licks you of his own accord. Once your pup understands how to respond to "lick-lick" you can begin to apply the cue as needed. When he nips say, "Eh-eh!" in a sharp voice. Your pup should pull back. Follow immediately with a happy-sounding, "Lick-lick!" and present your closed hand. Praise as he switches to licking.

Don't Leave Me This Way

Your wolfdog is a very social creature who loves to be with his family. You can use this to your advantage by using isolation as a punishment. Parents do this all the time with their kids—it is called a "time out." To give your pup a time out, use a verbal phrase such as "too bad" or "time out" at the moment he nips, then immediately take him to a time out area. If your pup is the type who considers the back yard Doggie Disneyland, it is not an appropriate time out area. If he is the type to sit at the door waiting forlornly to be let back in, the yard will do. A crate, assuming your pup is already accustomed to it, can also be used as a time out area. Don't worry, your pup will not begin to hate his crate, any more than your child hates his room because he is sent there.

Once you have placed your pup in the time out area, ignore him for two to five minutes. If he barks or whines, do not start counting time until he is quiet. When time is up, calmly let him out. You will find that the number of time outs needed might seem like a lot at first, but will quickly decrease.

If you are spending time with your pup in a gated area such as a kitchen or puppy pen, a time out can be administered by leaving the area. If he is tethered (attached by a leash to a couch leg or other sturdy piece of furniture), you can deliver a time out by simply moving out of range and ignoring him, then returning when time is up. The latter type of time out is more appealing to many people, as it is faster and easier to remove oneself than it is to remove a pup to a time out area.

The Bitter Truth

There are a variety of taste deterrent sprays on the market. These products are normally sprayed on furniture or other items to make them taste bad and thereby prevent unwanted chewing. The most commonly recommended brand is Bitter Apple™, but Listerine™ mouthwash can be used as well. *The product is never to be sprayed at the dog, since doing so could result in eye irritation or worse.* Instead, spray one finger of one hand. Interact with your pup as usual, using the other hand. When he bites down say, "Eh-eh!" and follow immediately by swooping the treated finger into his mouth, making sure the finger touches the tongue. The result should be your pup doing the canine equivalent of saying, "Yech!" and withdrawing immediately.

Your pup will soon come to associate the "Eh-eh!" with the distasteful sensation that follows, and the verbal "Eh-eh!" alone will become a conditioned punisher. That means when your pup hears it he will think *uh-oh, I know what comes next* and will stop nipping immediately; at that point the spray will no longer be necessary.

Whichever nip-deterrent method you employ, be patient and consistent. Your pup will soon grow out of this stage and into a well-mannered adult.

Jack kicks back

Digging

You might notice that there are no sections in this book titled "problem behaviors." That is because behaviors such as digging, chewing, and jockeying for social rank are *natural* for wolves and dogs; *they* do not consider them problematic. We, however, must learn how to modify those behaviors in our canine companions so they can live in our homes.

Digging is one of the most common complaints made by wolfdog owners. Wolfdogs dig to escape, to create cool resting places, to bury bones or other possessions, because they are bored, or because they simply enjoy the act of digging. But since you do not want your yard to resemble the surface of the moon, let's discuss ways to curb digging, or at least limit it to one spot.

Excavation Frustration

Because digging is a natural canine behavior, rather than trying to prevent it, why not give your wolfdog a "dig pit" where he can dig to his heart's content? Choose a small, out-of-the-way area of your yard that consists of soil or sand. To teach your wolfdog to dig there, have someone hold him on leash. (If that is not possible, tie him to a tree or fence for the moment.) Show him a favorite toy, treat or bone, and allow him to watch as you bury it; then release him. Naturally, your wolfdog will run directly to the area and begin to dig. Tell him in a happy voice what a clever wolfdog he is, and if you would like, help him dig up the treasure.

Repeat the buried treasure exercise a few times a day. Next, begin to bury goodies in the dig pit without your wolfdog's knowledge. When he digs there, surprise! It's The Most Rewarding Spot in the Yard! That ought to be all it takes to convince your wolfdog to choose the dig pit for his excavations. If you catch your wolfdog digging in an area that is off-limits, say, "Eh-eh!" and walk him over to the dig pit and encourage him to dig there instead.

If your wolfdog digs in inappropriate spots when you are not home, confinine him while you are gone. Either build a dog run (see *Containment*), or if he is accustomed to a crate and you are going to be gone for less than four hours, crate him indoors.

Don't Fence Me In

The first thing to consider if you have a wolfdog who tries to dig along the perimeter of your fence to escape is whether you are providing enough physical exercise and mental stimulation. Take your wolfdog for a long walk or play with him in the yard before you leave for the day. Right before you go, present your wolfdog with a long-lasting chew bone or a Kong™ filled with canned dog food and crumbled cookies or kibble. Kongs, available at most pet supply stores, are hard rubber balls shaped like snowmen. They have a tiny hole on top and a large one on the bottom. (See *Wolfdogs A-Z* for an entire section on Kongs and other great chew toys for wolfdogs.) Your fur-covered bundle of energy cannot be chewing and digging at the same time, and by the time he has finished chewing, he should be ready for a nap.

Some wolfdogs, even when provided with exercise and chew toys, will still dig to escape the confinement of a yard. These wily, wanna-be Houdinis dig right along fence lines, attempting to crawl under and out. One inexpensive solution to this type of digging has already been discussed in the chapter on containment. The Fido Shock™ system (or hot wire in general) is effective in stopping digging along the perimeter of your yard, since it keeps your wolfdog away from the fence line. The other solution for perimeter digging, also previously discussed, is to bury a skirting of chain link along the fence line. With either method, your wolfdog's attempts at digging will be effectively thwarted.

> *Like fence-jumping, digging out is a self-reinforcing activity. Once your wolfdog has successfully escaped, the drive to do so again is likely to be stronger. Strengthen your containment now so this behavior does not start in the first place.*

Random Acts of Digging

If your wolfdog digs at random spots in the yard rather than around the perimeter, place some of his feces in each hole, then fill the holes with dirt. That should stop the digging at those sites. Do the same for each new hole. With repetition, this technique will stop some wolfdogs from digging altogether.

Wolfdogs are extremely intelligent. If they know you disapprove of their digging, most will not do it when you are present. Watch your wolfdog from inside the house. If he starts digging, correct him verbally through an open window. You could even surprise him with a quick squirt from a water gun or garden hose you have attached to your kitchen faucet. But remember, your corrections must be timed to coincide exactly with the act. If you find a hole that has already been dug, it is too late to correct your wolfdog, as he will not associate the correction with what he has done.

One last thing to consider: since many wolfdogs dig in order to have a cool place to lie, be sure your yard has at least one comfortable, shaded area at all times of day. If you do not have trees, perhaps there is room to create a "den" under your back porch or other area. A dog house is another alternative to provide a cool, shaded area, assuming your wolfdog will go inside instead of just hanging out on top as so many do.

Sequoia relaxes in a cool, shaded area

Phantom stretches, relaxed as well.

Dominance Issues

Dominance

Dominance. The word is possibly one of the most overused when it comes to our relationships with dogs. What is dominance and what does it mean in regard to your wolfdog? It all begins with pack structure. In a wolf pack, there is an "alpha pair." This male and female are, as the song goes, *Leader(s) of the Pack.* They are normally the only pair to produce pups and are deferred to by other pack members. Beta is second in rank to alpha, and the hierarchy descends from there all the way down to omega. Dominance challenges are part of normal wolf behavior and are how pups, as they grow, find their place in the social order.

Two male wolves at Wolf Park "jaw sparring" for dominance. Neither wolf actually closes its jaws and the dispute is settled without violence.

The problem comes when we try to apply the wolf model to our human-canine pack. Normal puppy nipping and jumping are suddenly interpreted as a bid for dominance; in reality, those actions are perfectly normal, enthusiastic gestures from pups who do not yet know any better.

As pups enter adolescence and board the Hormone Express bound for sexual maturity, problematic behaviors may become more pronounced. Any parent of a teenage child can relate to the frustration that evolves as the previously dutiful child develops selective hearing and impaired compliance levels. Canine habits such as nipping and jumping, if not modified during the puppy years, can seem more threatening in adolescence because of the size of the dog, the energy behind the actions, and the dog's increased confidence level. As a wolfdog owner, your leadership status, consistency and patience will serve you well during the trying adolescent period, which lasts from roughly six months to two years of age.

An adolescent wolfdog who previously expressed a fear of people by running away might now start taking offensive measures such as growling, air-snapping or even biting. If that occurs, seek professional help immediately.

Alpha State of Mind

In your pack, *you* should always be the alpha—the top dog, the big kahuna, the undisputed leader. But good leadership does not involve yelling or being physically harsh. In fact, it is the middle-ranking members of a wolf pack who skirmish and jockey for position. The alpha has nothing to prove. Alpha ia a state of mind, a confident control. The best alphas are not likely to fight unless seriously provoked; they rule with a cool, assertive air of dignity. When the alpha corrects a pack member it is quick and decisive. All is then forgiven and peace is restored to the pack. This is the type of leader you should strive to be.

In wolf packs, body language and communication are so clear that skirmishes seldom turn into full-scale fights.

Leadership Program

Whether your wolfdog is a pup or an adult, he should be on a leadership program. On the following pages you will find gentle, non-coercive methods to help you establish yourself as leader of your pack. With practice, these exercises will become part of your daily routine. The program will produce a well-mannered pack member who knows his place and is more secure for it.

Leadership does not mean being a bully. *Never hit, shake, slap or use other harsh physical corrections; there is simply no need to do so.* Leading by force could produce a skittish, fearful animal who ends up biting you—and with good cause. A sharp verbal "Eh-eh!" is sufficient to interrupt the behavior of most canines, wolfdog or not. The dog can then be redirected to an appropriate activity, or if necessary, be given a time out. The best thing about employing a leadership program is that you will soon find that there is less and less need to correct your wolfdog in the first place.

Sit for It

Sit is an easy skill to teach. Begin with your wolfdog standing.
Hold a treat an inch or less in front of his nose. Keeping it at that
distance, move your hand slowly back and over his head. His
head should tilt up and back, tracking the movement. As his head
continues to move backward, his rear will hit the floor. When it
does, say "Yes!" and let him have the treat. The "Yes!" is a verbal
"marker" (sometimes called a "bridge") that lets your wolfdog
know the exact moment he is doing what you want. The verbal
marker is always followed by a treat. (Had you been clicker
training, you would have used a click in place of the "Yes!" For
more information on clicker training see *Resources* for *Clicking
with Your Dog*.) After three to five successful repetitions, add
the verbal cue by saying "Sit" right before you lure with the treat.
Once you have added the verbal cue, you can stop saying "Yes!"
when his rear hits the floor. You should still, however, continue
to deliver the treat as a reward.

Next, fade the treat as a lure by pretending it is in your hand as
you make the hand movement. When your wolfdog sits, reward
from the other hand. Your hand movement is now becoming a
hand signal to request that your wolfdog sit. If you prefer, you
may use an alternate hand signal: let your arm hang by your side
with palm facing forward, then bend the arm as though you were
lifting a dumbell. It may help to lean slightly forward as you give
the signal. Once your wolfdog is consistently responding to your
request to sit, help him to generalize by practicing in different
locations (indoors first and then outdoors), on different surfaces,
and with *you* in different positions, e.g., sitting, standing by his
side instead of facing him, lying down.

The Sit command can now be used as a valuable component of

your leadership program. Teach your wolfdog that when he wants something, he must earn it by doing something for you—in this case, sitting. Rewards that should be earned by sitting include food, treats, the door opening to go for a walk, a ball being tossed, and receiving affection.

At mealtimes, have your wolfdog sit for his food. Prepare his meal, say his name to get his attention, then say "Sit" and give the hand signal. If your wolfdog responds by sitting, praise him, place the dish on the floor and let him eat. If he does not respond immediately, count to ten silently in your mind. If he sits during the count, present him with the food. If you reach ten and your wolfdog is still not sitting, say, "You must not be hungry!" and walk away, placing the food in an area beyond wolfy reach. Return two minutes later and try again. Most canines, on the second try, respond with butt hitting ground in record time. That is because they are learning that there is a consequence for non-compliance. You will soon find that your wolfdog responds immediately during this sequence, and might even offer the sit before you ask.

Most wolfdogs love to receive affection. They solicit it from people by sliding up against us, pushing furry heads into our hands, pawing, whining, or staring with that adorable puppy-dog look. Who could resist? Of *course* you should give your beloved companion lots of affection—but not on *his* terms. If you do, he has trained you! You might not consider affection to be a reward, but if your wolfdog finds it valuable, why not use it as a training treat? When your wolfdog solicits affection, ask him to sit. Once he is sitting, bestow affection to your heart's content. As your companion learns other basic obedience skills, they can be used to earn your attention as well. For example, if your wolfdog is already sitting when he solicits affection, ask him to lie down and then pet him. You could even offer a nice tummyrub.

Just say No

In any social group, the one with the most power also has the most social freedom. Think of a wolf pack—or an office! The lower ranking members are the ones who scurry to and fro soliciting interaction and approval from higher ranking pack members. The higher ranking, when solicited, will sometimes comply and sometimes not; it is their choice. You, as alpha of your pack, have the most social freedom. To demonstrate that power, respond every now and then to a solicitation for play and/ or affection with "not now." ("Every now and then" means once or twice out of ten times, not half the time.) Simply look at your wolfdog, say, "Not now" once in a calm voice, then fold your arms and look away, to the side and up. Hold the pose until he walks away. Soon your saying "not now" will result in his giving up and walking away immediately. "Not now" can also be used by your guests.

I taught my German Shepherd, Soko, "not now" when she was a pup. Now eleven years old and still ball-obsessed, she will still try once in a while to engage me in ball-throwing while I am eating dinner. I have never complied in all these years, so I cannot explain her persistence—I suspect she is a Border Collie in a German Shepherd's body. When she solicits the game I ignore her and continue my meal until I cannot stand being stared at any longer. I finally turn to her and say, "Soko, not now." She responds by picking up her ball, walking to her dog bed, and collapsing on it with a huge sigh. What a drama queen!

Controlling the Good Stuff

Parents control resources that are valuable to their children. These include allowance, curfew, and playtime. Controlling valuable resources is an effective way to convey to your wolfdog that you are in charge.

Food One of the most valuable resources as far as your wolfdog is concerned is food. For that reason, it is better to feed twice daily than to leave food available at all times. If you leave food down, your wolfdog will perceive it as coming from that amazing round thing that is always magically full. Contrast that with the food being presented by you, Oh Great Controller of Good Stuff, twice daily, along with a request to sit first. (Water is also extremely valuable but should be available at all times.)

Play If your wolfdog enjoys playing tug or chasing a ball, those games can be used as rewards. In most families, the wolfdog brings the toy to the person, and the obedient human complies. Who's in charge? Instead, keep the Sacred Play Object hidden away. Whenever *you* would like, take it from its hiding place and offer to play with your wolfdog. Or at the least, when your wolfdog presents the item, ask for a sit before you engage in play. Now you are also the Source of Fun!

Access to Location Lots of people like their wolfdogs to curl up on the couch with them; some even encourage them to share the bed. Others feel that wolfdogs have no place on beds, furniture, or anywhere that belongs to the "alpha." Some wolf behaviorists theorize that being higher physically equals being higher in rank, and therefore allowing a wolfdog on raised surfaces in your home sends the wrong message.

Whether you allow your wolfdog up on furniture is a personal decision. But whatever you decide, be consistent and retain control. If you have decided you do not want your wolfdog on the furniture, give him a comfy dog bed of his own and offer lots of attention when he lies on it. Make sure that all family members follow the rules—there always seems to be one "untrainer" in the family! If you would like to allow your wolfdog up on the couch, teach him that when you are sitting on the couch he must ask permission to join you by sitting, then waiting for your okay. If you do not want to allow him up at the time say, "Not now." It might be necessary to body block him the first few times you refuse his request. You may also find it helpful to place a blanket on the couch and teach your wolfdog that he is allowed up only when the blanket is present. This trick comes in handy when traveling or visiting friends.

Your wolfdog should also be taught to respond to "off," meaning to remove himself from furniture. Start by standing with your side facing the couch. Move your hand in a downward, sweeping motion from couch to floor while saying, "Off." If he does not comply, gently help him down. Be careful about grabbing your wolfdog's collar, as many canines do not appreciate that gesture and might snap or bite. If necessary, snap on a short leash to move him, then consult a professional regarding handling issues.

Doorways Access to location is not limited to furniture. Your wolfdog should not be allowed to knock you aside and blow through doorways, nor to dart out the front door. You control those locations. There are two ways to teach that concept: One is to put your wolfdog on a sit-stay, open the door, go through, then either call him to come or give a release word. (A release word is a word or phrase that tells your wolfdog that he is "off duty," that the command or training session is over. Choose a word other than "okay," as it is often used in conversation.) The sit-stay method can be used at the door leading to your yard, at the front door, and when loading your wolfdog into or out of your vehicle.

The other way to teach waiting at doorways is to use body blocking. Position yourself near the door, facing your wolfdog. Without saying a word, open the door. When your wolfdog moves forward, block him as though you are a hockey player trying to block a goal. You can even walk into his space so he is forced to move back. When he gives up and stands and waits, release him to go through. Be careful when attempting this method if you have a large, powerful wolfdog who outweighs you! If practicing at the front door, attach a long line to your wolfdog's collar with the other end secured around a heavy piece of furniture.

Space Invaders As he lopes along, a high ranking wolf may give a gentle "hip bump" to lower ranking wolves who are foolish enough to stand in his way. Since you are the leader, your wolfdog should not be allowed to encroach on your space. If your wolfdog crowds you, use your lower body to gently move him away. This should not to be confused with kicking the poor animal! Use your knees, thighs or hips (depending on your wolfdog's height) to push him away. If you are sitting, use the area between your elbow and shoulder (or elbow and wrist if it is more comfortable) to move him away. Do not make it into a game—the gesture should be smooth and firm.

Another common space issue involves doorways. Many canines seem to enjoy lying across them, thereby controlling foot traffic in and out of a room. If your wolfdog is blocking access to where you want to go, say, "Excuse me," and keep both feet on the floor while shuffling gently into him. He will quickly learn that "Excuse me" is his cue to get up and move. If this method is not effective with your particular wolfdog, move back a few feet, call him to you, praise, then walk on by.

The bottom line in a leadership program is that there must be clear communication and consistency in ground rules. In the best of all worlds, a leadership program would be established when your wolfdog is a pup. But even if you adopt an adult wolfdog, the same rules can be applied. Depending on the individual, you might have to take it a bit slower. Give lots of rewards for good behavior and use common sense. For example, if your wolfdog growls when you block his path, do not force the issue. Walk away and act disgusted. Then take a moment to assess his behavior and if necessary, employ the help of a professional.

The Testosterone Factor

Although there is some disagreement in scientific circles as to the behavioral effects of testosterone, one thing has been established: male canines who have not been neutered are at higher risk of developing male-male dog aggression issues. For that reason alone, neutering your male wolfdog makes sense. Your female should also be spayed, since you are not a professional breeder and there are already way too many unwanted wolfdogs.

There is much anecdotal evidence that unaltered wolfdogs are more likely to challenge their owners, especially during adolescence and into early adulthood. Neutering does not guarantee that your wolfdog will never challenge you; but it could help, and might also discourage marking behavior (raising a leg and leaving a lovely yellow calling card.) Intact wolfdogs are also more likely to get what is referred to as "winter wolf syndrome," a crankiness that manifests around breeding season and can include severe dominance challenges. Winter wolf syndrome is *not* something you want to go through if it can be avoided. One wolfdog owner I know had a great relationship with his high content fur-kid—except in the winter, when he could not even enter the enclsoure for fear of being attacked.

Neutering drastically lowers the chance of certain cancers in both sexes, and in males, greatly reduces that Roaming Romeo behavior when a neighborhood female is in heat.

Dealing with Challenges

Although you might not ever have to deal with your wolfdog challenging your authority, it is best to know how to respond should a challenge occur. One safe, simple response is to remove yourself from the area, making it apparent that you are disgusted. You can even utter a disgusted, "Ugh!" as you stalk off. Ignore your wolfdog for two to five minutes. You are delivering a time out, a mild punishment for unwanted behavior. An alternate way to respond, if you feel it is safe, is to lead your wolfdog to a time out area. (Attach a leash rather than attempting to drag him by the collar.) Leave him alone for two to five minutes, then allow him back in and show him you still love him. Wolves do not hold grudges and neither should you.

Your leaving the area, by the way, does not mean that your wolfdog has "won the challenge." You are showing leadership by delivering a calm, decisive response, rather than making your already upset wolfdog more so. Shouting or responding physically will only arouse your wolfdog further—and you do *not* want to wrestle an agitated wolfdog! Strive to gently diffuse the situation while maintaining your composure. With patience and consistent leadership, these challenges should become less frequent. If you decide to consult a professional, interview carefully so you can choose one who understands how to address challenges gently without using harsh physical corrections.

The Alpha Roll

There is no tactic so hotly debated and so firmly entrenched in the wolfdog world as the *alpha roll*. This supposed display of human dominance is commonly performed by forcing the wolfdog onto his back and holding him there until he submits. Some owners growl and stare as they do so. I have heard of at least two owners who also bite the wolfdog's nose or neck! You might have guessed by this point that I do not recommend this type of technique.

In a wolf pack, one wolf might display dominance by placing his teeth around another's muzzle. The wolf on the receiving end submits by rolling over on his back—*voluntarily*. He is not being forced! The notion that wolves correct each other by using an alpha roll type of maneuver is based on an old, faulty wolf study. We know better now.

The other common misconception (and popular justification for using force) is that adult wolves roughly roll or shake young pups. This simply does not happen in nature. Furthermore, do you really think if you tried it that your wolfdog would believe he was being corrected by another wolf? Your attempted communication might well lose something in the translation.

Safe Alternatives

Can you assert your dominance without implementing an alpha roll? You betcha! I'm a 5 foot 2 inch, petite female. Every one of the male wolfdogs at the rescue center outweighs me, and they are all certainly stronger than I am. Over the years I have been challenged by a few. So what's a girl to do? One tactic is vocalization. Your voice is a more powerful tool than you know. Once when I uttered a low, forceful *"No!"* to a wolfdog who would not stop jumping on me (he had to be a Timberwolf/ Energizer Bunny hybrid), he dropped to the ground and looked up as if to say, "Did that come out of *you*?" With over-enthusiastic jumpers, I turn my body slightly to the side, letting them fall to the ground on their own. I then praise and pet when all four paws are on the ground. If they get seriously obnoxious I will say, "Too bad!" and leave the pen, conveying the message that pushy behavior equals loss of playmates. (In your home, an alternate way to prevent jumping would be to teach your wolfdog to sit for attention. After all, he cannot sit and jump at the same time.)

There is no magical, across-the-board solution for dominance issues. Each situation is different, as is each wolfdog. Establish leadership using the methods outlined in this section, never respond to a challenge with violence, and if necessary, consult with a professional behavior specialist. Above all, be kind, patient and consistent—be a good alpha.

Children and Wolfdogs

When parents decide to add a dog to the family, they envision it romping happily with the children, spending evenings curled up with the family, and maybe even protecting the children. But any canine, wolfdog or not, also has the potential to harm a child. The higher the wolf content, the less suited a wolfdog will be to living with children. Of course, there are exceptions. But if you are the parent of a young child and are trying to decide whether to get a wolfdog, please consider a dog instead. There are many child-friendly dogs in shelters who are literally dying for a good home. And there are northern breed mixes who have wolfy looks without the accompanying risks. If you already have a wolfdog and are the parent of a young child (or have visitors who are young children), please read this section carefully and implement the suggestions so that all parties can interact safely.

You might be wondering why am I so adamant about child/ wolfdog safety issues. Wolfdogs are large, extremely strong animals. They can cause damage to a child without meaning to by knocking them down in enthusiastic play or by jumping up in greeting. Many wolfdogs, especially the higher contents, have a more highly developed prey drive than the average dog. That instinct increases the potential risk of an attack being triggered by a small child's running, screaming, or falling down and crying. And because wolfdogs become aroused quickly, unsupervised rough play could quickly escalate into something more serious.

Never leave *any* child unsupervised with a wolfdog, even if that child knows how to behave around the dog. It takes mere seconds for an accident to happen, and when wolfdog/child incidents happen, they can be very serious.

What to Teach Children

1. *Approach and Petting* It is important that your children understand the right way to approach and pet your wolfdog. Many children will approach a dog with hand extended, palm-down over the dog's head. This motion can be perceived by the dog as threatening; a pup might raise his head and nip, while an adult might display behavior such as growling or snapping. Initial petting should be focused on the wolfdog's chest and the side of the face, without leaning over him. As the wolfdog becomes comfortable, children may move to the top of the head and the back. Monitor for signs that your wolfdog is becoming uncomfortable. Common signs include stiffening of the body, "hard eye" or getting up and moving away. Teach your children to recognize those signs and to respond by slowly moving away. Encourage kids to move slowly during any interaction with the wolfdog. They should do their best to refrain from making startling sounds or movements, and should never stare him in the eye.

2. *Never hit, poke, pull, slap, kick, shake, roll or try to ride the wolfdog!*

Also, never hug the wolfdog tightly; while humans see this contact as pleasant, canines perceive it as restraint, which is threatening. Many young children, especially girls (girls love to hug), are bitten in the face while hugging dogs.

3. *Never try to take things away from the wolfdog.* That includes food, bones, toys, or a child's possession that the wolfdog has grabbed. If the wolfdog has been taught to drop objects on command, teach your child to use that command. (There is a sequence showing how to train the drop command on the *Train Your Dog* DVD—see *Resources*.) If the wolfdog has not yet been taught to drop objects on request, teach your child to call you any time the wolfdog has grabbed something. If *you* are having trouble getting something valuable or dangerous away from your wolfdog, in a pinch, use bribery. Run to the refrigerator and grab a handful of yummy treats; scatter them on the floor. When your wolfdog goes to investigate, he will drop the object.

4. *Let sleeping dogs lie.* Never startle a wolfdog who is asleep. Some canines have a strong startle reflex and will automatically snap at anyone who disturbs their rest. If your wolfdog is asleep and your child wants to wake him, your child should call the wolfdog's name first (along with clapping hands or stomping feet in place if necessary), then approach when he is fully awake.

5. *Don't run and scream* when playing around the wolfdog. I know, it is much easier said than done to get a child not to run and scream. But as previously mentioned, this combination can trigger prey drive. If you have a wolfdog who tends to chase and jump on your kids when they run, tether him during playtime, using a leash or steel-coated cable. Give him a chew bone to help keep him busy. That way he can be around the kids while they play without interfering or putting anyone at risk. Whenever possible, have child/dog interaction time when both parties are pleasantly worn out.

6. *Do not play tug-of-war or rough-house* in any way with the wolfdog. While tug games are fine for older children and adults

to engage in with the wolfdog (as long as the person remains in control), young children should not be permitted to play these games. Tug can quickly escalate into overzealous pulling and lunging that could result in injury. Also, the wolfdog might try to regrip the tug toy and clamp down on the child's hand instead.

Rough play such as wrestling is something that human males in particular seem to enjoy. Wrestling is not, however, an appropriate activity for children to engage in with wolfdogs. If you find that the mouthiness your wolfdog employs in wrestling with an adult is beginning to carry over to other people and situations, the wrestling should be discontinued immediately.

7. *Never hit your wolfdog.* Your children should be taught that it is not their place to punish the wolfdog. If the wolfdog is doing something wrong, they should call for parental assistance immediately. Older children (depending on the child and the dog) may deliver a reprimand using a sharp, loud "Eh-eh!" along with a hand clap. The startling sound is usually enough to stop canines in their tracks.

8. *Jumping* When wolfdogs jump on kids, most kids flail their arms, or run and scream. That in turn excites the wolfdog further— the game is on! Unfortunately, this sequence can be dangerous for kids and also rewards the wolfdog for jumping. That reward increases the odds that he will continue the unwanted behavior. Teach kids to respond to jumping by "being a tree." That means turning to the side, folding their arms and standing still. If the wolfdog sits, they may then calmly interact with him. Chances are, when confronted with a human tree, your wolfdog will wander off. After all, his playmate seems disinterested in his invitation to play. If the "tree" method does not work, parents should intervene and redirect the wolfdog to another activity.

9. *Be aware of canine body language*. When interpreting canine body language, it is important to observe the dog as a whole. You can, however, teach children what common canine body postures and gestures mean. Yawning or licking of the lips often indicates stress. Of course, dogs yawn and lick their lips at other times, but stress signals are usually fast, repetitive gestures. Stiffening of the body, hard eye, curled lip, growling, snarling, or raised hackles are a definite warning. Ears pinned back against the head and tail tucked usually indicates fear. *Teach kids that approaching a fearful dog who feels cornered can be extremely dangerous!* Tail carriage and movement can also be indicative of a dog's emotional state; just be sure to take your dog's normal tail carriage into account when making interpretations. In general, a dog whose tail is wagging in a relaxed swoop parallel to the ground is happy. If the tail is held high and wags stiffly like a flag, it could indicate dominance or even be a precursor to aggression. A tail held low, wagging quickly could indicate nervousness, excitement, or submission. Teach your child that if she is unsure of what the wolfdog's body language is saying but feels apprehensive in any way, to call for you immediately.

What to Teach Your Wolfdog

There are many things your wolfdog should learn in order to be a good pack member, including basic obedience and manners, bite inhibition, to share resources, and to accept physical handling. Here are a few specifics to teach your wolfdog in order to keep your children safe:

1. *No jumping up on people*. Teach your wolfdog to sit to greet people. After all, he cannot be jumping and sitting at the same time. No one should pet the wolfdog until he is sitting.

2. *Others may handle your food.* Although children should be taught to leave dogs alone while they are eating, you must also "people-proof" your wolfdog around food. Do not isolate your wolfdog at feeding time. If you do, he might eventually become possessive of food, the bowl, or even the feeding area. Sift your fingers through his food as he eats, petting and speaking to him softly. You could even hand-feed him bits of food. Make it enjoyable!

Once you are sure your wolfdog is comfortable with your being near his food, have your child approach and drop small bits of cheese or hot dog in the dish as you stand by. The treat should be something more valuable than your wolfdog's food. The child should remain upright and not bend forward to dispense the treat. This exercise will teach your wolfdog that children coming near his food is a good thing. If you notice any body language that indicates discomfort or aggression, stop immediately and reassess the situation. Use caution. If you have just taken in an adult wolfdog, keep your children away at mealtimes and when he has bones or other resources, until you have had time to assess your new pack member's behavior.

3. *"Settle"* This verbal cue comes in handy when play has turned rambunctious, or whenever you want your wolfdog to relax and mellow out. Teach it when your wolfdog is relaxed. Have him lay down, then gently help him onto his side as you say "settle" in a soothing voice. He should be expected to remain in the lying position for only a few seconds at first. Practice a few times daily, gradually building duration. You could practice while watching television, reading, or working on the computer. Once your wolfdog is doing longer settles, have your children practice with him. When he has mastered the skill, whenever your kids feel overwhelmed by him they should, as calmly as possible, ask him to settle.

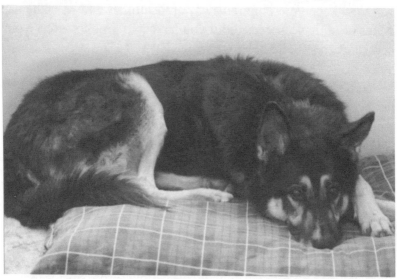

Mojo, low content German Shepherd/Mal/Rottie/wolf mix

The "Home Alone" Wolfdog

Wolves are extremely social creatures. It is very difficult for any canine, whether wolf, dog or wolfdog, to spend extended periods of time alone. Unfortunately, many of us have obligations and do not have the luxury of spending all day with our companions. If you are away from home a lot, it is recommended that you provide your wolfdog with a canine companion.

Playing Matchmaker

An appropriate companion for your wolfdog would be a dog of similar size, of the opposite sex. (There is less of a chance that canines of the opposite sex will fight than will same-sex pairs.) This buddy does not need to be a wolfdog; the two will still understand each other's body language and communication. Of course, both canines should be altered (spay/neutered).

Another important consideration in match-making is temperament. For example, a very dominant wolfdog should not be matched with another who also has an alpha temperament. A submissive companion would be a better choice in that case.

Interior Decorating 101

Many people leave their wolfdog inside the home while they are gone, only to discover that their four-footed friend has been hiding a talent for interior design! The couch looks *so* abstract chic with that hole through the middle, and isn't the linoleum much more interesting with the corners pulled up? Some low and mid content wolfdogs can be left in the house unsupervised without incident; most high contents cannot. Many owners of wolfdogs, even low and mid contents, wisely choose to confine them to the yard when they must be left alone. Destruction, however, is not limited to the indoors. Many a wolfdog owner has come home to find siding missing from the house and flower beds redone in the ever-popular "moon crater" motif. Building a sturdy pen or enclosure might be necessary. (See *Containment.*)

Echo, low content Malamute/wolf mix

Separation Anxiety

Some owners believe their home-alone wolfdog has "separation anxiety," an anxiety that manifests when the dog is left alone. Dogs who have true separation anxiety may chew or claw at doorways, whine, drool, bark incessantly, and even injure themselves. As a canine behavior specialist, I find that the majority of owners who call with this complaint turn out to have dogs who are simply bored and destructive because they are left alone for hours on end. If you cannot alleviate that boredom and loneliness by providing your wolfdog with a canine companion, take heart. There are still ways to make the daily separation easier.

Your wolfdog should be introduced to being left alone gradually. Think of it this way: as a child, if your parents left you alone for an hour while they went to the market, you might be a bit nervous. But with reptition, you would soon learn that when your parents leave, they return. If they then left for a few hours to visit friends, you might be a bit anxious, but you would already have experience on which to base the expectation that they will return. If they continued building separation time slowly, by the time they left for a day trip or overnight stay, you would be confident that you had not been abandoned. Now imagine instead that your parents never took those short initial trips. How would you feel if, after being doted upon and having spent all day with your parents, you were suddenly left alone for two days? You might panic; at the least, you would experience some level of anxiety. It is no different for a wolfdog pup, or even an adult rescue in a new home.

Many people bring their new companion home on a weekend so they can spend some quality time with him before returning to work on Monday. But all that undivided attention followed by suddenly being left alone all day is hard on a wolfdog. Use whatever get-acquainted time you have to get your wolfdog accustomed to short separations. Leave your companion in his pen or wherever he will spend time when you are gone. (Get your companion used to being left in his pen for short periods when you are at home first.) Do not make a big deal when you leave. Choose a phrase such as "See you later!" and say it casually whenever you leave. Keep your arrivals low-key as well.

At first, keep the separations short. The first few times, leave for five to fifteen minutes. You could drive around the block or do quick errands such as putting gas in the car or visiting a bank machine. Gradually build up the length of the absences to a few hours. Soon your wolfdog should be used to longer separations and be less anxious when you are gone.

> *Another way to reassure your wolfdog when you are gone is to leave a radio or television playing. Assuming you normally play the radio or television when you are home, the sound will have become associated with your presence.*

Smells Like Mom!

To give your wolfdog extra reassurance while you are gone, leave something with your scent on it such as an old t-shirt or sweatshirt that you have recently worn, or a towel that you have rubbed under your arms. If your wolfdog is left crated, the item can be used as bedding in his crate. If he is left loose in the house, he could use the item to curl up on. If your wolfdog is in a pen and you do not want him to destroy the item, leave it close to the pen, but not so close that it can be dragged in by long, limber legs.

Distraction Action

Giving your wolfdog something to do immediately after you are gone, in the form of an interesting chew item, can help immensely. Doing so will not only give your wolfdog a positive association with your leaving, but will give him something to do in that crucial just-after-you-leave Destructo Period. Get a Kong™ toy and stuff it well, or use a long-lasting chew bone you know your wolfdog likes. (Another one to try is bully sticks, also sold under the name pizzle sticks.) As you leave, present the chew bone. Don't be insulted if your fur-child doesn't even look up as you leave! Most likely, after working at the bone for a while, your wolfdog will take a nice, non-destructive nap.

If the Worst Happens

If you return home to find major destruction, do not punish your wolfdog. Punishing any dog after the fact will only confuse and scare him, as canines do not associate things that happen more than a few seconds apart. Let's say your wolfdog tore up a prized rug during your absence, at 10:00 a.m. You return home at 5:00 p.m. and yell at your wolfdog. The problem is, he does not know why you are yelling at him! If you repeat this sequence often enough, your wolfdog will come to fear your return, since you always seem to be angry when you enter the house.

Instead of punishing your wolfdog, quietly clean up the mess. Take a moment to calm down, then think logically why the destruction might have occurred. You might need to reconsider where your wolfdog should spend time while you are away. Pups under two years of age are not normally reliable in the house alone, and neither are high content wolfdogs. Consider the circumstances, and set your wolfdog up to succeed.

DIET/NUTRITION

Most wolfdog owners feed a diet based on dry kibble, and most believe their chosen brand is a healthy one. And why shouldn't they? If we are to believe television commercials, there are dog foods that can make your companion not only healthier, but younger! *Suuure* there are—and none of us have a single wrinkle because there is truth in advertising, right ladies? Whether it is cosmetics or dog food, you must learn to read ingredient listings to get the real facts.

Become Label Able

As a general rule, most dog foods sold in supermarkets are of poor to fair quality. It is worth the expense and the trip to a pet supply store to purchase a higher quality kibble. Think of it this way: the money you invest now might well save you hundreds of dollars in veterinary care down the line.

Wherever you obtain your wolfdog's kibble, read the label carefully. All pet food labels must, by law, list ingredients in descending order of bulk weight. Chicken and turkey based foods are well tolerated by many wolfdogs. Look for a food that lists a whole meat source such as chicken, turkey, lamb or beef as the first ingredient. If a meat source is followed by the word "meal" it is not necessarily bad, but is not as high quality as the meat source listed alone. A meat source followed by the word "by-product," however, should not appear high on the list of ingredients. By-products are parts of animals that are not nutritionally useful. Chicken by-products, for example, include beaks and feet.

Corn is another ingredient that should not appear high on the list. Corn is a grain to which many canines are allergic. This allergy commonly manifests as dry, itchy skin. Some canines, wolfdog or not, can also have allergies to other ingredients such as wheat flour or soy. Ideally, the first two ingredients listed should be high quality meat sources. Corn and soy, if they appear at all, should be low on the list.

Check toward the end of the list to see which preservatives have been used. The label will say "preserved with..." Choose a food that lists natural preservatives such as Vitamins C and E. Avoid any brand that lists ethoxyquin, BHA, BHT, propylene glycol, or sodium nitrate. Those are the "bad preservatives"—some are actually known carcinogens.

Another section of the label breaks content down into percentages of protein, carbohydrates, fats, fiber and moisture. While you might choose a high protein food for a very active wolfdog, do not base your food choice solely on these figures, as they can be misleading. After all, shoe leather has a protein content, but you wouldn't want that "29% protein" to be derived from it! The combination of animal and grain sources in a dry food is listed as "crude protein." You must take into account the bioavailability of the food (ability to be used by the body), which translates to your wolfdog finding the protein from chicken or beef more useful than that derived from shoe leather.

Many owners complain that their wolfdog has that anorexic supermodel look and is seemingly unable to gain weight. A lack of good bioavailable ingredients in the kibble is often the culprit. (Another cause of wolfdogs not being able to keep weight on is worms—see *Health Concerns*.) There are many excellent quality kibbles available that do not contain corn, soy, or toxic preservatives. A few are Innova, California Natural, Canidae, Wellness and Wolf King. Wolf King's meat sources are bison and salmon, which makes it a good choice for wolfdogs who are allergic to other meat sources. If your wolfdog is a pup, he should be fed a kibble specifically formulated for pups. Puppy foods are higher in protein and other ingredients needed by growing pups. If your wolfdog is elderly or has medical issues, consult your veterinarian regarding his specific nutritional needs.

Simba and Vincent,, two high content pups

Do Wolfdogs Need Meat?

One of the most commonly asked question regarding wolfdog nutrition is whether they need meat in their diet. If you define need as "need it to survive," the answer is no. It is entirely possible for even pure wolves to survive on a quality, high-protein kibble. But there are many wolfdogs, especially high contents, who do not seem able to tolerate a kibble-only diet. Some develop chronic diarrhea, while others cannot maintain weight.

If you choose to feed meat, you can either use it to supplement a kibble-based diet, or feed what is known as a "raw food" diet. The most common raw food diet goes by the acronym BARF (Bones and Raw Food, or Biologically Appropriate Raw Food). A proper BARF diet consists of meat and meaty bones, pulverized vegetables, various items such as eggs and yogurt a few times weekly, and supplements. While feeding this way requires effort, there is much anecdotal evidence that raw diets may be responsible for curing everything from skin and coat problems to disease. There is some concern regarding the dangers of dogs choking on bones. For that reason, some wolfdog owners grind the meat (bones and all) to ensure safety. For more information on the BARF diet refer to Ian Billinghurst's *Give Your Dog a Bone* (see *Resources*) and the many informative BARF sites on the internet.

If you decide to supplement or base your wolfdog's diet on meat, a good staple is chicken necks and backs. *Do not boil them!* Boiling could cause the bones to splinter, which could render them fatal when ingested. Although many wolfdog owners have fed raw chicken necks and backs for years with no problems, some veterinarians caution against salmonella poisoning. If you are concerned (especially if you have young children who might handle the meat by accident), an alternative would be to boil turkey or chicken and feed the meat alone.

Many wolfdog owners boil kidney, heart or liver as a supplement. Organ meats can be obtained through a butcher or supermarket. Choose natural, free-range meats whenever possible, as toxins are highly concentrated in organs such as the kidneys and liver. Do not overfeed organ meats—a few times a week is plenty. *Note: There is no truth to the old wives' tale that feeding raw meat will make an animal aggressive. Spouses, however, may become grouchy if you cook more often for the wolfdog than you do for them!*

Organ Meats as Tasty Treats!

1. Bring organs to a boil
2. Set aside to cool
3. Cut into 1/2 inch slices
4. Bake at 250 - 300° or until they look dry
5. Cool and serve sparingly

Spirit loooves organ meats!

Stool Sleuths

Signs of a healthy wolfdog include a shiny coat, clear eyes and stools that are firm and well-formed. Become a "stool sleuth" so you can monitor your wolfdog's health. Abnormal stools can be an indicator of anything from worms or digestive upset to more serious health issues. One common cause of canine diarrhea is switching abruptly from one food to another. To switch to a new brand of kibble, mix the new food in gradually.

Gradual Transition to New Food:

Days 1-3	1/4 new food, 3/4 old
Days 4-6	1/2 new food, 1/2 old
Days 7-9	3/4 new food, 1/4 old
Day 10 & on	new food only

Picky Eaters

Some wolfdogs are very picky about their kibble. If your wolfdog refuses to eat the high-quality kibble you have so diligently researched, try pouring chicken broth over it. To make it even more enticing, heat the broth first. Or try VitaGravy, a gravy-like supplement with vitamins that comes in a bottle resembling salad dressing. You could also try mixing in a healthy brand of canned food. Whatever you add, mix in the extras *before* presenting the meal. If you offer the dry food alone first, then add tasty extras after the dry has been refused, your wolfdog will quickly learn that refusing food earns tasty additions.

The fact is, no dog will starve himself. If your wolfdog does not eat within ten to fifteen minutes, remove the food. He will soon learn that he has a limited amount of time in which to eat, and will soon start eating meals when they are offered.

For further information on canine nutrition, refer to *The Holistic Guide for a Healthy Dog* by Volhard & Brown, and *Dr. Pitcairn's Complete Guide to Natural Health for Dogs and Cats*. (See *Resources*).

Heyoka coaxes kibble out of a hard Jolly ball that has had holes drilled to make it into an interactive food toy.

Health Concerns

Most dog breeds have genetically based health concerns specific to that breed. Wolves do not. Therefore, the breed of dog in a wolfdog mix can suggest potential health problems. For example, because German Shepherds have a high incidence of hip dysplasia, a wolfdog who is mixed with German Shepherd will be at higher risk for developing hip dysplasia than would one who is mixed with Husky.

Get to a Vet!

Do not take anyone's word for it that your new wolfdog is in good health. Take him to a veterinarian immediately for a thorough checkup. If your breeder or rescue group has supplied vaccination records, bring the papers along. Bring a stool sample as well, so it can be examined for worms and parasites. Worms are a common problem in pups and are the reason some wolfdogs cannot seem to maintain an appropriate body weight. Although tapeworms are easily seen in stool, many other worms and parasites are invisible to the naked eye. Your veterinarian will view the stool sample under a microscope to make a diagnosis.

Do not list your companion as a wolfdog on veterinary records. Whatever the dog breed, state that instead. For example, if your wolfdog is a malamute mix, list him as such. You might be proud of his being part wolf and want the world to know, but listing him as a dog mix is for his own safety. Even if wolfdogs are currently legal in your area, that could change at any time. Do not deny his wolf heritage to your vet; just *don't put it on paper*.

Vaccinations

All canines should be vaccinated, including wolfdogs. They must be inoculated against distemper, hepatitis, leptospirosis, parvo and parinfluenza. The vaccination given to prevent these diseases is called the DHLPP or "6-in-1." Vaccinations should be started early in your pup's life. The first vaccination is normally given at four to five weeks of age, with boosters following every two to three weeks up to 14-16 weeks of age.

At the age of 16 weeks, your wolfdog should receive a rabies vaccination. Because of legalities, some vets will not administer the rabies vaccine to wolfdogs; this should not be confused with the vaccine being ineffective on wolfdogs. If your vet will not accomodate your request, find one who will. Rabies is fatal, and being inoculated against it is especially important for a canine who is likely to chase squirrels and other potential carriers of the disease. The other reason it is important to have your wolfdog vaccinated against rabies is that in the event that he bites a person or dog, producing paperwork that proves he is current on his rabies vaccination could save his life.

Anesthesia

There is some disagreement in the wolfdog community as to whether anesthesia affects wolves and wolfdogs differently than it does other canines. Many veterinarians claim the amount of anesthesia needed per pound is exactly the same in wolfdogs and dogs. On the other hand, some owners have testified that they actually lost their beloved wolfdog to an overdose of anesthesia— the same amount that would have been safe for a dog. If your wolfdog must be put under general anesthesia, check with your vet that the safest type of anesthesia will be used. Ask for it to be administered at a low, consistent level throughout the surgery rather than given in one large initial dose at the start.

Care should be taken with medications as well. Some wolfdogs are very sensitive to drugs. When administering drugs such as tranquilizers, start with a low dosage. Keep in mind that stress can affect how a wolfdog reacts to drugs. A stressed animal might fight the drug, giving the appearance that it is not working; but adding more and more of the drug could prove fatal. Administer *any* medication when your wolfdog is calm. I have seen cases where ace promazine, a drug often prescribed to calm canines for short periods such as car trips, had the opposite of the desired effect because it was given when the wolfdog was already stressed.

The Pre-Exam Visit

Trips to the vet can be stressful for any canine. Wolfdogs who are naturally shy and sensitive can be particularly frightened. If possible, bring your wolfdog to the vet well before your scheduled appointment. Let the office staff know ahead of time that you will be making brief visits to help get your companion comfortable with the environment, and visit at times when the office is not likely to be crowded.

When you enter the vet's office, act relaxed and happy to be there. If the staff is not busy, ask someone to feed your wolfdog a treat that you have brought along; if they are busy, feed it to him yourself. Then take him home. These brief visits will help to form a positive association in your wolfdog's mind and will go a long way toward making actual exams easier. Wolfdog owners should also simulate at home things that their companion will experience at the vet (e.g., restraint, examination of ears and mouth) so as to lessen the stress of the actual visit.

It is unfortunate that a veterinary exam is often the catalyst that causes an owner to realize that her wolfdog has an objection to being handled in certain ways. Many a vet tech has been bit while trying to restrain a dog. Early desensitization to handling is the best way to avoid this problem, but if that has not been accomplished, two things should be done: get your wolfdog accustomed to wearing a muzzle for brief periods so he can wear one during veterinary exams; and work on desensitizing him to being handled. Both of these should be addressed under the guidance of a professional trainer.

An Ounce of Prevention

Always keep your veterinarian's phone number handy, along with the phone number and address of the nearest emergency clinic. *Do not assume that you will remember the information when it is needed.* Panic impairs the ability to think and to remember facts. Posting the number on the fridge is helpful. Another number to keep handy is the ASPCA National Animal Control Center's Poison Hotline, 1-800-548-2423. This is a 24-hour service that can prescribe treatments for different types of poisoning. There is a $25 charge for the call. That might sound like a lot, but it would not seem like much if your beloved companion were in danger.

Get a book on pet first aid and keep basic supplies on hand. When treating injuries, what applies to dogs applies to wolfdogs; just use caution and go slow when handling your wolfdog. Pet first aid courses are available through the American Red Cross.

Above all, if you suspect that something is wrong with your wolfdog, take him to the vet immediately. It is always best to err on the side of caution.

Tips n' Tricks

Here are some tips and tricks to make daily life with your wolfdog run a bit more smoothly:

Giving pills Many dog owners administer pills by opening the dog's mouth wide, shoving the pill to the back of the throat, then shutting the mouth and stroking the throat to stimulate the swallow reflex. That might work well with your wolfdog. But if your wolfdog has such well-developed canines that the traditional method would not be conducive to keeping your fingers intact, there are other ways. Join me, won't you, in the Wolfdog Owner's Mantra: "Hot dogs are my friend." That's right, you can easily stuff most pills into a hot dog. Most wolfdogs, well, *wolf* hot dogs down so quickly that there is no time to discover the pills, especially if you toss the hot dogs so they must be caught in mid-air. For wily wolfdogs who spit out the pill, prepare four pieces of hot dog. Toss the first, the second, the third (with the pill in it) then the fourth, in rapid succession. This ruse is enough to fool most wolfdogs, especially if you alternate in which piece the pill is placed. Alternate methods include hiding the pill in canned food, sprinkling it over canned food after crushing with mortar and pestle, or wrapping it in cheese or liver paste.

Water Buckets Wolfdogs are notoriously destructive. If they are not eating the water bucket, they are tipping it over. It is important for canines to have access to fresh water at all times. If your wolfdog lives in a chain link enclosure or you have chain link fencing, clip a metal bucket to the chain link. Using a metal two-sided clip, hook both the bucket handle and the chain link through the same clip loop. Attach the other end of the clip to the chain link for added stability.

Another option is to get an extremely heavy plastic bucket or horse trough, or even a used porcelain sink. (Don't laugh, we did it at the rescue!) Or dig a hole and bury the bucket so that it cannot be tipped. There are also automatic waterers such as the types that attach to horse corrals, and gadgets that can be attached to your outdoor faucet to deliver water when a lever is pressed.

Smoke (mid-content) shows off his handiwork

Cool Dogs Fill a round, shallow plastic container with water. Wedge a hot dog halfway down, then freeze. Before you leave for the day, present your wolfdog with the resulting tasty ice block. Many wolfdogs will lie or roll on these blocks, while others crunch through quickly to get to the hot dog. Placing ice cubes in your wolfdog's water dish is a good way to keep his water cool; even if he tips the bowl, he can still lick the cubes.

Tips Worth The Price of This Book Keep garden hoses out of reach! Seems like common sense, doesn't it? But just about every wolfdog owner I know has lost numerous garden hoses before realizing just how long their lithe companion's reach could be. If your wolfdog spends time in a pen, be sure the hose is well out of reach. If he is left free in the yard, store the hose at an entirely different location. For wolfdogs who eat sprinkler heads, place a square of hardware cloth over the head (allowing enough room for it to pop up), then tack down with long spikes on each corner.

Applying Ointments and Creams Many owners who have attempted to apply cream or ointment to their wolfdog can attest that it is not an easy feat. A common dilemma is how to apply creams to prevent fly bites, which are commonly found on the ears of wolfdogs who live outdoors. Getting the cream *on* the wolfdog's ears can be challenging, especially if your fleet-footed friend sees it coming. Having trained your companion to accept this type of handling from puppyhood is best, but if that is not the case, here are two tricks to try:

1. Hide the cream. Transfer some cream into a smaller, uncapped vial and hide it in your clothing—women, putting it down the front of your bra works well! As you pet your wolfdog, surreptitiously dip into the ointment and work it into the afflicted areas.

2. This one takes advantage of the wolf's natural inclination to scent-roll and is especially helpful for those "untouchable" types. Wipe the ointment on a log, the side of a doghouse, or anything else your wolfdog could rub up against. Most will immediately begin to scent-roll head-first on the new, enticing stuff. It will probably get all over them in the process, but most should end up on their head and face area.

Wolfdogs in the Car Some wolfdogs do fine in the car. Others do not enjoy car rides, and some will even vomit and/or defecate. The key to introducing your wolfdog to the car is to do it in small increments and make it a positive experience. Open the door or hatchback of your vehicle and coax your wolfdog inside with a treat. (Can you hear the Wolfdog Mantra?) Do not start the car. Sit inside with your companion, offer a few hot dogs and praise, then let him out. Repeat a few times.

Next, coax him inside and turn on the engine. Keep the engine running while giving treats and praise, but do not actually drive anywhere. This allows your wolfdog to acclimate to the vehicle's sounds and smells while a good association is being created by pairing them with tasty treats. When you feel your wolfdog is comfortable, take a short trip. Once around the block is fine at first. Progress gradually to longer trips, making sure they have a pleasant destination. In other words, the first few trips should end at a park where your wolfdog can romp or a friend's house where he receives treats and praise—not at the vet's office to be neutered. If you plan to have your wolfdog ride crated in your vehicle (the safest method), crate train him first. Then introduce him to the vehicle as described above, but put the crate in the vehicle first, then coax him into the crate.

If Your Wolfdog Becomes Lost Always keep a current ID tag on your wolfdog. It should state your phone number, an alternate phone number (such as your vet's) and "Reward for Return" on the reverse side. Your wolfdog should be microchipped as well. Many dog owners do not see the need for a microchip until their dog's collar and tags come off while he is out running the streets. If someone were to find your wolfdog and was able to approach him, they might bring him to a nearby shelter where he would be scanned for a microchip and you would be contacted.

Search your local shelter at least once every few days. Look in the medical area as well as the adoption pens. Ask about the shelter's policy regarding how long strays are kept before being put up for adoption or euthanized, so that you know exactly how often to search. Do not expect shelter workers to tell you by phone whether your wolfdog is there; you must go in and look yourself.

Keep a current photo of your wolfdog on hand. Not only will it come in handy to prove ownership if your wolfdog is brought to a shelter, but it can also be used to create a "lost dog" flyer. Do not use the "w" word (wolfdog) on the flyer, but rather, his dog breed mix, e.g., "Husky mix" or "Malamute mix." Post flyers at all area shelters, vets' offices and groomers.

Give a copy of the flyer to your local postal worker and other service professionals who regularly cover your neighborhood. Offer neighborhood kids a reward for spotting your lost dog. Place ads in local newspapers. Do daily walking searches of your neighborhood, calling your wolfdog's name. Wolves and dogs are crepuscular, meaning they are most active at dawn and dusk, so search during those times. If your wolfdog has a canine companion, bring him along on the searches. Most importantly, don't give up hope! Many canines who are lost turn up weeks or even months later. People sometimes take in a stray dog, then bring them to the shelter a few days or even weeks later. Some canines turn up at shelters far from their original starting point, so search as many shelters in your surrounding area as possible.

Sit to Greet Visitors Wolfdogs are extremely energetic and agile creatures. Unfortunately, that can translate to overly enthusiastic greetings that can knock a child, or even an adult, off her feet. Teach your wolfdog to sit to greet people. Attach his collar to either a leash or a tether that is attached to a solid piece of furniture.

Tell visitors that as long as the wolfdog's rear is on the ground, they may approach and greet him. If he stands, they should turn to the side, fold their arms, and stand still. Once he is sitting again, they can resume their approach. I know one person who threw a pizza and beer party where the price of admission was to help teach the wolfdog proper greetings! The more chances your wolfdog has to practice this exercise, the more quickly he will become accustomed to sitting to greet. The leash or tether will soon become unnecessary. Use daily walks to your advantage as well. If someone wants to pet your furry friend, explain that you are training and to please pet him only when he is seated.

Potty on Cue Whether your wolfdog is a pup or an adult, it is helpful to establish a verbal cue that lets him know that you would like him to urinate. This cue comes in handy during the housebreaking phase, saves time when you travel, and is a great help when you are standing in a downpour waiting for your wolfdog to go already! To establish the cue, bring your wolfdog to his normal potty area. Starting first thing in the morning is best, as most canines urinate soon after waking. When he begins to circle and sniff (a precursor to urination in most dogs), gently urge, "Go potty." Be sure to use a soft, coaxing voice rather than a loud, sharp tone so as not to startle him. When he has finished, praise. After a week or so of repeating the exercise a few times daily, test your wolfdog to see whether he responds to the verbal cue. If not, a bit more practice is needed. If he does respond, offer him praise and give yourself a pat on the back. Well done!

Don't Shave! No, not you, your wolfdog! Many owners of heavy-coated breeds shave their dogs in the summer in the hopes of alleviating heat-related discomfort. Many wolfdog owners are tempted to do the same, since their fur-kid is mixed with Malamute or Husky. Don't do it! A dog's coat helps to regulate his body temperature; it keeps him warm in the winter and cool in the summer. That fur coat also guards against sunburn. If you must, clip the coat short, but do not shave it entirely.

Marking Many male wolfdogs, upon reaching adolescence, begin to raise their leg and spray urine on vertical surfaces. This marking behavior is the canine equivalent of leaving one's calling card. If your wolfdog is still intact, the best way to solve the issue is to have him neutered. While neutering is not guaranteed to stop marking behavior, it is often sufficient. If your wolfdog still marks after having been neutered, apply the same solutions you would for any housebreaking issue.

Keep Your Sense of Humor That might seem like a strange tip but believe me, a sense of humor will go a long way when your wolfdog has chewed your third pair of running shoes or is standing there grinning, half your dinner hanging out of his mouth. You made the decision to share your life with this intelligent, problem-solving, lovable bundle of energy, so take it all with a wolf-sized grain of salt. Train him, socialize him, love him, and don't sweat the small stuff.

"Bye! Don't forget the tummyrubs!"

RESOURCES

Recommended Reading/Viewing

Dog Language: An Encyclopedia of Canine Behavior
Abrantes (Denmark)
Denmark: Wakan Tanka, Inc., 1997 ISBN 0-96604-840-7

Give Your Dog a Bone
Ian Billinghurst
N.S.W. Australia: Billinghurst, 1993 ISBN 0-646-16028-1

How to Teach a New Dog Old Tricks
Ian Dunbar*
Oakland, CA: James & Kenneth Publishers, 1991 ISBN 1-888047-03-8

* Ian Dunbar's books may be purchased through most Barnes & Nobles
and Borders book stores, or ordered directly from the publisher at James &
Kenneth Publishers, 2140 Shattuck Avenue #2406, Berkeley, CA, 94704,
(510) 658-8588.

The Other End of the Leash (human/canine body language)
Patricia McConnell, PhD
New York: Random House, 2003, ISBN 034544678X

The Dog Whisperer
Paul Owens
Hollbrook, MA: Adams Media Corp., 1999 ISBN 1-58062-203-8

*Dr. Pitcairn's Complete Guide to Natural Health
for Dogs & Cats*
Pitcairn and Pitcairn,
Emmaus, PA: Rodale Press, 1995 ISBN 0-87596-243-2

Don't Shoot the Dog
Karen Pryor
New York: Bantam Books, Inc., 1984 ISBN 0-553-25388-3

On Talking Terms with Dogs: Calming Signals
Turid Rugaas
Kula, HI: Hanalei Pets, 1997 ISBN 0967479606

Tellington TTouch
Linda Tellington-Jones, 1992-2003
(Various books and videos are available. Go to amazon.com or dogwise.com and search for Ttouch. It is an excellent method of massage to relax your wolfdog and get him used to handling.)

Clicking with Your Dog
Peggy Tillman
Waltham, MA: Sunshine Books, 2000 ISBN 1-890948-05-5

Holistic Guide for a Healthy Dog
Volhard & Brown
New York: Macmillan, 1995 ISBN 0-87605-560-9

Wolfdogs A-Z: Behavior, Training & More
Nicole Wilde
CA: Phantom Publishing, 2000 ISBN 0-9667726-1-X

Train Your Dog: The Positive Gentle Method (DVD)
Producer: Leo Zahn
Featuring Nicole Wilde and Laura Bourhenne
Available through www.picturecompany.com
ASIN: B0000800VO

Book Sources

Dogwise (formerly Direct Book Service)
(many excellent pet-related books) 1-800-776-2665
www.dogwise.com

Wolfshadow Books
Hard to find/out of print wolf-related books; write for catalog.
WolfShadow Books, 200 Route 46, Mine Hill, New Jersey,
07803 or call 973-366-5780

Association of Pet Dog Trainers (APDT)
Search for a trainer in your area.
www.apdt.com or 1-800-PET-DOGS

Products

Nature's Miracle™   310-544-7125
Anti-Icky-Poo™   1-800-745-1671
Tethers   dogwhispererdvd.com/products.htm

Wolf Centers

International Wolf Center   Non-profit educational
1396 Highway 169   org. Environmental ed.
Ely, Minnesota 55731-8129   about wolves. Resident
(800) ELY-WOLF   pack. Research expedi-
www.wolf.org   tions, "wolf weekends."

Mission: Wolf   Captive-born wolves and
P.O. Box 211   wolfdogs. On-site educa-
Silver Cliff, CO 81249   tional programs, traveling
(719) 746-2919   "ambassador wolf."
www.missionwolf.com

Wild Canid Survival
and Research Center (WCSRC)
P.O. Box 760
Eureka, MO 63025
(314) 938-5900
www.wolfsanctuary.org

Cares for endgangered
wolves. Educational
programs, Adopt-A-Wolf
program. Gift shop,
mail order catalog.
Visitation during open
season.

Wolf Haven
3111 Offut Lake Road
Tenino, WA 98589
(800) 448-9653
www.wolfhaven.org

Sanctuary for displaced
wolves. Open to the
public. Wolf Haven takes
a harsh view of wolfdogs
as pets. Write for more
info on programs.

Wolf Hollow
Route 133
Ipswich, MA 01938
(508) 356-0216
www.wolfhollowipswich.com

Wolf Hollow is a non-
profit educational facility.
Dedicated to teaching and
providing an opportunity
to experience the wolf in
as natural a setting as
possible. Offers educa-
tional seminars on site.

Wolf Park
Battleground, IN 47920
(317) 567-2265
www.wolfpark.org

Dedicated to research and
public education on
behalf of the wolf. See
wolves at close range,
view wolf-bison
demonstrations, hear
lectures. Offers seminars,
practicums, internships.

Wolf Song of Alaska
P.O. Box 110309
Anchorage, AK 99511-0309
(907) 346-3073
www.wolfsongalaska.org

Non-profit organization. Emphasis on wolf education and sciences. Internationally acclaimed wolf exhibit, education center and gift shop. Internship /volunteer programs are available.

Wolf/Wolfdog Rescues

Wolfdog rescues come and go. Rather than trying to include all current rescues and chance giving obsolete information, included below is only Wild Spirit Wolf Sanctuary (formerly Candy Kitchen), the best established wolfdog rescue center. Carefully research any organization to which you choose to donate, and give generously to the legitimate ones. Theirs is no easy task.

Wild Spirit Wolf Sanctuary
(Candy Kitchen Rescue Ranch)
Star Route 2 - Box 28
Ramah, NM 87321
(505) 775-3304
www.inetdesign.com/candykitchen

Open to the public rescue facility for wolfdogs. Does educational outreach. Sponsorship programs available. Boards wolfdogs.

Wolfdog Registries

Iowolfer Association, Inc.
2517 Franklin Avenue
Mt. Pleasant, Iowa 52641
www.iowolfer.org

Lupine AWAREness
P.O. Box 461
Landing, N.J. 07850
www.lupineawareness.org

USAWA
P.O. Box 663
Williamstown, NJ 08094
www.nb.net/~usawa/

Internet Resources

www.inetdesign.com/wolfdunn (The Wolf Dunn)
www.searchingwolf.com (The Searching Wolf)
www.wolfpark.org (Wolf Park)

For general information about wolfdogs, go to any search engine (e.g. Google, Yahoo) and type in wolf, wolfdog or wolf hybrid.

Internet Mailing Lists

By e-mail subscription. No fee to join. After subscribing, you will receive posts by all list members as e-mail. Some lists are high volume; you could end up with as many as 100 e-mails a day.

Wolfdog List Subscription instructions at Wolf Dunn web site.

To find other groups, visit http://groups.yahoo.com and search for wolf hybrids or wolfdogs.

Train your Wolfdog with Nicole Wilde!

Train Your Dog
The Positive Gentle Method

DVD

92 minutes

Producer

Leo Zahn

Featuring professional trainers Nicole Wilde and Laura Bourhenne, this interactive DVD guides you step by step using real, untrained dogs (including a wolfy malamute!). Use the handy menu to click on obedience exercises, puppy issues, manners (includes not jumping on people, not nipping, and taking food gently). Clicker training. Plenty of bonus materials. You will be amazed at how fast your wolfdog learns!

These methods are ideally suited for teaching wolfdogs.

Go to picturecompany.com for full description, video clips and ordering information.

So You Want to be a Dog Trainer

Have you thought about becoming a dog trainer but didn't know how to go about it? Get step-by-step instructions and inside tips from a professional trainer. Topics include getting an education; setting up your business; advertising; group classes; in-home sessions; phone tips; safety tips; products and more.

172 pgs. paperback

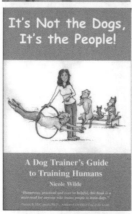

It's Not the Dogs, It's the People!

Any trainer can tell you that the hardest part of dog training is training the owners! This humorous, helpful book covers dealing with difficult personality types; family dynamics; working with kids; group class considerations; handling sticky situations; and much more.

132 pgs. paperback

One on One
A Dog Trainer's Guide to Private Training

Selling single sessions vs. packages; taking a history; sample phone scripts; designing lessons plans and protocols; much more. Bonus section with ready-to-use forms, contracts and handouts.

All books by Nicole Wilde. Available through dogwise.com, amazon.com and your local book retailer.